Adrift Without My Anchor

BOOKS BY CARIN SEALS

Becoming My Own Anchor Journal
Unanswered Questions No More Journal

Adrift Without My Anchor

My Personal Journey of Love, Loss & Grief

CARIN SEALS

Dedication

For my mother,
who gave everything she had so her children could have more.
Who taught us to be resilient without ever saying the word. Who loved
us through storms and still managed to leave sunshine behind.

I didn't always understand your choices,
but I see now—you were doing the best you could
with what you had, and you did it with fierce love.

Thank you for keeping us together,
for never letting go,
and for planting that mustard seed of faith in us
that still grows to this day.

You are missed in every moment,
remembered in every breath,
and carried in every word of this book.

You always told me,
"What comes from the heart touches the heart."
My prayer is that this book does exactly that
touches, blesses, and reaches every heart that needs it.
This is for you, Mommy.
You will never be forgotten.

Love always,

Carin

Library of Congress Control Number: 2026935317
Book Cover Concept by Carin Seals
Book Cover Design by Capture Your Brilliance LLC
Editing by Heidi Siebels
Layout by Capture Your Brilliance LLC

ISBN Paperback: 979-8-9941957-0-3
ISBN eBook: 979-8-9941957-1-0

Contents

A Message for Others Who've Lost a Loved One 1

Introduction - When the World Went Quiet 5

Guidance 9

1. The Silence After Love 11

2. After the Scales Fell 19

3. Healing Through Her Story 25

4. When Faith Had to Carry Me 31

5. Transitioning Back Home 43

6. Love Day 51

7. When Grief Is Loud 61

8. Living in the Silence 67

9. Support Systems and Letdowns 73

10. The Unspoken Weight of Being the Strong One 79

11. Rebuilding Through Routine 87

12. The Guilt of Moving On 93

13. Honoring Her Life Every Day 99

14. Light in the Shadows...105

15. Life Goes On, So Will I...111

The Journey Continues..117

Acknowledgements...119

A Message for Others Who've Lost a Loved One

If you're holding this book and you've lost your mother, mother figure, or another loved one, I want to say this first:

I see you.

I see your broken heart.

I see the way you smile on the outside while collapsing inside.

I see how strong you've had to be—stronger than you ever wanted to be.

And I'm so sorry.

It is okay to feel it all: the sadness, the anger, the guilt, the relief, the confusion, and the longing. Your grief is real, even if your relationship was complicated—even if you thought you wouldn't grieve them at all.

Healing doesn't mean pretending it didn't hurt, or that everything was perfect. It means finding a way to make peace—with what was, what wasn't, and what will never be. It means allowing yourself to honor their life in whatever way feels true to you, while also honoring your own story and your own growth.

There is room for your love, your pain, your questions, and your healing here.

I know what it feels like to wake up and forget for a split second that they are gone—only for the truth to crash over you like a wave.

I know what it feels like to hear something funny and instinctively reach for your phone to call them, only to remember you can't.

I know what it is to walk into a room and feel the ache where their presence used to live, whether that ache comes from missing their presence—or from the fact that you never really had their presence to begin with.

And I know what it feels like to wonder if you'll ever feel whole, or at peace, or free from the weight of it all.

You may never feel exactly the same as before.

But you will feel different.

You will find new strength.

You will find new ways to carry them with you—or to make peace with the pieces they left behind.

Please know this: there is no one way to grieve.

Not on a timeline. Not in a straight line.

It's okay to be a mess.

It's okay to cry over a scent, a song, a piece of clothing.

It's okay to laugh and feel guilty—and then remind yourself that joy is allowed.

It's okay to feel nothing at all one day, and completely undone the next.

Your grief is yours, and however it shows up—it's valid.

You're not failing.

You're not broken.

You're grieving.

And in grief, love never dies.

It transforms. It moves from presence to memory, from voice to echo, from touch to legacy.

If you're wondering how to go on, start here:

One breath at a time.

One small joy at a time.

One day of allowing yourself to feel—and *not* be okay.

You are not alone.

I wrote this book for you.

To walk beside you, not ahead of you.

To tell the truth about the pain, but also the power that rises from it.

Because we are not just grieving children or loved ones.

We are the legacy-bearers.

The light-keepers.

The storytellers.

The ones who carry our mothers, fathers, loved ones forward in every beautiful, complicated, courageous step we take.

So even now, even in your sadness, I want you to repeat this:

I am still hers (theirs).

And she is (they are) still mine.

Death did not end our love—it only changed the way we share it.

You will make it through this.

Not perfectly.

But honestly.

Softly.

Bravely.

And when you do—you'll be someone else's light, too.

Peace and blessings,

Carin Seals

When the World Went Quiet

Inhale……Exhale….. Repeat. Inhale……Exhale…..Release.

E ach breath I take is a quiet reminder that I am still here—still learning how to exist in a world that feels unfamiliar without my anchor.

For me, an anchor represents stability, strength, and faith. It is what holds you steady when the waters rise and the storms come without warning. My mother was my anchor. She grounded me when life felt chaotic, steadied me when I drifted too far, and reminded me who I was when I began to forget myself. She wasn't just the woman who gave me life—she was my constant. My cheerleader. My safe place. My peace in the middle of chaos. When life broke me, she helped hold me together. When doubt crept in, she spoke truth over me.

But I also know that not everyone's story looks like mine.

Maybe your birth mother wasn't your anchor. Maybe she carried wounds of her own that made it hard for her to love the way you needed. Maybe she placed you for adoption. Maybe you grew up in foster care. Maybe you were raised by a grandmother, aunt, cousin, or family friend who stepped in and gave you what they could. Or maybe your anchor wasn't your mother at all—but a person who showed up through wisdom, guidance, patience, or unconditional care. However they entered your life, their presence mattered. And their absence—left an imprint.

It wasn't just my mother's absence I grieved—it was the silence that followed. The kind that echoes in rooms she once filled with laughter. The kind that creeps in late at night when I just want to hear her voice say, "It's going to be okay, baby." But she couldn't say it anymore. And I wasn't okay.

When an anchor is lost, it isn't just the person you grieve. It's everything connected to them. For some, that means losing the closest bond they've ever known. It's the conversations you'll never have again. The advice you can no longer ask for. The comfort you leaned on. The version of yourself that existed when they were still here.

For others, it's the weight of unspoken words, unmet expectations, unanswered questions, and dreams of a relationship that never happened. Even if your relationship was complicated, strained, or unfinished, their absence can open wounds you didn't know were still tender, reminding you not only of what was lost but of what you longed for and never had the chance to heal.

Grief is strange. It doesn't ask permission. It shows up unannounced, sits on your chest, and dares you to get up. I didn't write this book to explain grief. I'm not sure anyone can. I wrote this because maybe you're here too, trying to steady yourself after losing your anchor, that one person who kept you grounded when life's storms threatened to pull you away.

This is a story of love, loss, pain, and also a story of rising. Of choosing to live—even when I didn't want to. It's about healing that doesn't happen all at once, and how love never truly leaves us, even when the ones we love do.

If you've lost your mother, mother figure, or special loved one—especially if they were your anchor—you already know that the world transforms in a way you can't prepare for. But I want you to know, page by page, through lessons I've learned, strategies that worked for me, and journal prompts to guide you through your own grief, you can heal. Slowly. Quietly. Gently. And one day, even joyfully.

Guidance

This book is designed to be *interactive*—a space for you to not just read, but to *feel, reflect, and release.* Healing is an active process, and this book invites you to participate in your own restoration. At the end of each chapter, you'll find journal prompts to help you process your thoughts and emotions. You can write directly in the book or use a separate journal if you prefer more space to express yourself. There's no right or wrong way to do this—just your way.

Write openly. Write honestly. Write freely.

Your healing is connected to your willingness to be truthful with yourself. The more you allow your heart to speak, the more you'll uncover the peace waiting within you.

Remember, this is not about perfection—it's about *presence*. Some days you may write paragraphs; other days, just a sentence or a few words. That's okay. Healing doesn't follow rules—it follows truth.

I've spoken from my heart in these pages, sharing my journey with raw honesty and faith. My hope is that as you read, reflect, and write, something within you begins to shift. Because what comes from the heart, touches the heart.

Take your time. Give yourself grace.

You are healing—one breath, one page, one prayer at a time.

- ONE -

The Silence After Love

M y relationship with my mother wasn't always easy. As a child, I remember watching families on television and quietly wondering why my life didn't look like theirs. Why couldn't my mother be that put-together? Why couldn't my home feel that stable? I wanted my mother to be like Claire Huxtable from *The Cosby Show*. She had a career and still managed to maintain her household by cooking, cleaning, and being supportive of her children. She was her daughters' role model, and they looked at her with utmost respect and admiration.

Instead of growing up with the idealized version of Claire Huxtable as my mother, my reality was very different. My mother was a young single woman raising five children. For the first ten years of my life, my anchor wasn't even my mother—it was my Nanny, my maternal grandmother. She was my protector, my nurturer, the one who filled in the gaps when my mother couldn't. Nanny's presence was reliable, her love a steady force. She gave me structure and the kind of love that was consistent, the kind of love a child could count on—while my parents struggled with addiction.

Nanny's house was home. My siblings and I lived with her most of the time, except when my mother periodically had her own place, and we stayed with her occasionally. Nanny was not an affectionate or an "I love you" kind of woman, but she showed me what unconditional love looked like through her patience, protection, and caregiving. She was not financially rich, but enriched us with her unconditional love. Nanny protected me from the drug-filled lifestyle of my parents.

Nanny was the cornerstone of my faith. It was through her that I discovered God, learned the meaning of faith, and understood the power of prayer. I attended Sunday School and youth night every week. I was on the junior choir and junior usher board. Prayer was my Nanny's answer to every problem. She taught me morals, discipline, and respect for myself and others, especially adults. I always had to address adults as Mr. and Ms. So and So. When any adult spoke, I had to listen and not talk back. I was not allowed to be present when "grown folks" were having conversations. Family problems and secrets were kept from us children. The model around her house was: "Stay in a child's place." She ran a tight ship in her household and did not have to physically harm us with her hand or belt. Everyone loved her and enjoyed coming to her house. She never passed judgment or turned her back on any of her nine children, even throughout their drug addiction and incarceration. She made sure every one of her grandchildren was in a safe environment and had a place to call home. My obsession with Nanny was ridiculous. She couldn't even go to the bathroom in peace without me at the door.

Then, one day, Nanny was gone—my protector, my safe place, the one who filled in the gaps when my mother couldn't. In an instant, the person who had been my shelter was no longer on this earth. I had so many questions for God. My ten-year-old mind couldn't begin to grasp why he would take her at just 54 years old. She still had so much love, so much wisdom, so much more to give.

———————

It was August 4, 1993, and I had been away at Rangerette camp for a week when a family friend came to pick my cousin and me up early. I was immediately confused when I saw her. When I asked why she was picking us up early, she avoided my question, simply urging me to get in the car. But the sadness in her eyes told me she knew more than she was willing to say. I refused to move until she told me the truth. Finally, with hesitation but no sugarcoating, she said the words that shattered my world: *"Nanny passed away."*

I couldn't process it. Her words bounced around my head like an echo, refusing to land. *Passed away?* Did she mean gone—like no longer on earth gone? Did she mean that when I walked back into Nanny's house, she would no longer be there to greet me, to listen to me excitedly share all the details about camp, because she knew I had been nervous to attend? My body instantly went numb, and my mind went into overdrive, clinging desperately to the idea that this couldn't be true.

Then I ran. Literally. I bolted into the woods, not caring where I was going, not afraid of anything in front of me. At that moment, the woods felt safer than the truth. Safer than standing there letting those words sink in. If I just kept running, maybe it wouldn't be real. Maybe I wouldn't have to face the fact that the woman who raised me, who loved me more than anyone else in the world, was gone—and I didn't even get to say goodbye.

After I emerged from the woods and returned to the car in complete tears, I was embraced by my cousin with a bear hug for comfort. We didn't verbally say anything to each other, but deep down, we knew that from that moment onward, our lives would change drastically. The drive home was heavy with silence. The kind of silence that presses against your chest, that makes the sound of your own breathing feel too loud. Through the silence, our tears kept coming, streaming down as if they carried all the words we couldn't form.

My Nanny was the first person I ever lost who truly meant the world to me. She had been my one constant from the moment I was born until the day she left this earth. Her funeral was a blur. I remember somehow finding the strength to speak at her funeral, sharing my love for her and expressing the deep gratitude I felt for having her in my life. I also remember refusing to look at her body in the casket. I didn't want that image etched in my memory. Instead, I held on tightly to the warmth of her love and the security she gave me. Saying goodbye that day was one of the hardest things I've ever done, and even then, I knew her absence had carved a void in me that could never be filled.

Losing Nanny changed me. I was still just a kid, but I felt like I had been forced to grow up overnight. My mother was so deep in her own grief that she couldn't be there for my siblings and me emotionally. No one asked me how I was feeling or coping. Therapy was never even mentioned—around that time in our family and community, therapy wasn't something you talked about. So, I had to deal with it and brush my feelings aside and just keep going.

But, throughout my life, Nanny's love stayed with me. She had poured so much into me that I refused to let her down. I used the pain of her passing to push me. To stay focused. To try to become the person she always believed I could be. Looking back now, I realize I put so much pressure on myself to get everything "right," to fix what was broken in my family, to succeed in a way that would make her proud. I neglected to give myself grace. Grace is permission to be human, to stumble, to not have all the answers. It's the gentle reminder that healing is not linear and that perfection was never required of me in the first place. Grace says, *"You're allowed to rest. You're allowed to hurt. You're allowed to grow at your own pace."*

For so long, I carried the weight of responsibility like it was the only way to prove my worth. But grace teaches me that my worth isn't tied to my performance, my ability to hold everything together, or my capacity to make others proud. My worth simply exists—because I exist. And that truth is something I wish I had learned earlier, something I am still learning even now.

My Precious Lessons

The First Loss Shapes the Heart.

Losing Nanny was my first real introduction to grief, and in many ways, it set the tone for how I handled loss for years to come. I learned to be strong, to keep going, to hide my pain so no one else had to carry it. At the time, I thought that was what strength looked like.

I've come to understand that Nanny's death shaped my determination and my resilience, but it also left me with a habit of holding everything in. That habit would serve me in some ways—keeping me focused, disciplined, and driven—but it would also keep me from fully feeling, fully processing, and fully healing for years.

Nanny's love still guides me today. When I feel like giving up, I hear her voice. When I question if I am enough, I think of the way she looked at me, like I was her world. And even though her death left a void that can never be filled, her life planted the roots of my strength—roots that would carry me through every heartbreak, every trial, and every season of loss that came after her.

Gems Along The Way

The things that helped me heal during my time of grief that may also help you are:

- **Faith foundation:** The prayers and spiritual teachings Nanny gave me became my anchor long after she was gone.

- **Holding on to memories, not regrets:** Choosing to remember her laughter, love, and presence, instead of focusing on her absence, helped me carry her with me.

- **The power of grace:** I had to learn that I didn't need to "perform" my way into worthiness or perfection. Grace allowed me to breathe, to be human, and to heal at my own pace.

- **Finding meaning in pain:** Instead of letting grief consume me, I used it as motivation to live in a way that honored her belief in me.

Journal to Healing

Take a moment to sit with what you've read in this chapter and reflect on your own journey. Allow the truth to gently rise to the surface. Let this be a space where your grief is allowed to exist—just as it is. In your journal, write your thoughts freely, openly, and honestly—without judgment, without pressure. There are no wrong answers here, only truth waiting to be realized

1. Who in your life has been your "safe place" the way Nanny was for me? How have they shaped who you are?

2. How do you carry the love and lessons of those you've lost into your daily life?

3. Where in your own grief do you need to extend yourself more *grace*—permission to hurt, to stumble, to rest, and to grow at your own pace?

- TWO -

After the Scales Fell

After Nanny's death, the scales fell from my eyes, and the life she tried to shield me from became a stark reality. In that moment, I felt akin to Eve after she had taken a bite of the forbidden apple; her eyes opened to a new world, and so did mine. I returned from camp to the same house, only this time it underwent an overnight transformation. I was exposed to a whirlwind of chaos, drugs, theft, family drama, and long-hidden secrets that all surfaced at once. The loss of My Nanny, my shelter, and my protector left me vulnerable and exposed to the harsh realities of the world I had been shielded from before.

Overnight, my mother had to face the reality that she had five children. Five children who were now depending solely on her. She could no longer come and go as she pleased or rely on her mother to pick up the pieces. She was faced with a choice—keep living in addiction and risk losing her children to the system, or fight for her own life and for her children. By God's grace, she chose to fight. She faced her battle with drug addiction head-on and won. That choice changed everything—not just for her, not just for her children, but for everyone who had the pleasure of connecting with her.

During this time, my mother's focus was on staying clean and holding life together—making sure there was a roof over our heads, food on the table, and clothes on our backs. Survival was her priority, but in that struggle, she didn't have the time or emotional energy to truly get to know her children on a deeper level.

Still, I longed for more. I longed for closeness, for the kind of mother-daughter bond I imagined other girls had. Instead, I carried resentment. We bumped heads a lot. I blamed her for her past choices and held her accountable for wounds she could no longer undo. I shamed her in my heart for her struggles and constantly compared her to the perfect image of Claire Huxtable—a standard she was never meant to meet. In doing so, I never gave her the chance to simply be my mother, to love her for the imperfect, resilient, and deeply human woman she was.

By the age of 16, I felt like my mother was harder on me than she was on my older sister. When my older sister left home, the responsibility fell on me—the next in line. Suddenly, I wasn't just a child anymore; I became the caretaker. I had to watch my younger siblings, wash the clothes, do the dishes—even when I hadn't dirtied a single one. At the time, it felt unfair. I couldn't understand why my mother treated me differently, why she seemed to see me not as her daughter, but as another adult expected to share and carry the load with her. I remember lying awake some nights feeling angry, exhausted, and unseen—wondering what I'd done wrong to deserve such expectations.

My friends would meet my mother and instantly fall in love with her. They thought she was hilarious—her openness, her bold honesty, her ability to make everyone around her feel seen and heard. She had this rare gift of connection; even strangers felt comfortable enough to share their personal life stories within minutes. She could walk into a room and shift the energy just by being herself—raw, real, and unapologetically authentic. Everyone else could see it so clearly, that magnetic light that drew people in. But for me, it was harder. I was too close to her story, too entangled in the pain and expectations between us to see her the way others did. While others saw her humor, I saw her exhaustion. Where they saw strength, I saw survival. It took me years—and grief—to realize that what others saw in her was real. I just couldn't see it then because I was still looking at her through the eyes of a daughter who wanted something more.

I remember reading a quote once that said, "You'll never realize how strong your mom was until you become her in a different season." In that moment, I brushed it off, convinced I was doing everything in my power not to become her. But God has a way of humbling us. Sure enough, around the age of 28, after I gave birth to my daughter, those words came back to me. The very things I swore I would never do, the same promises I spoke out loud, I found myself repeating with my own child.

Life had broken me down and forced me to see the world through a different lens—I began to truly see my mother. Not as the woman I wished she had been, but as the woman she actually was. A woman who carried more than most would ever see, who loved in ways that didn't always look or feel like love—but a love that never failed to show up, steady and unconditional. I started to recognize that the same boldness and honesty that drew people to her were also her armor. It was how she protected herself from a world that had rarely been kind to her. She wasn't tough because she didn't care; she was tough because she had to survive. And beneath that toughness was a heart that ached to protect her children, even if it wasn't always received how we needed. Once I saw her as a woman first—before the title of "mother"—I could finally understand her, forgive her, and love her more completely than I ever had before.

I began to understand that sometimes, mothers are hardest on the children they see themselves in. It's not always fair, but often, it's a reflection of their own unhealed wounds—wanting you to "do better" than they did, or protect you from what hurt them. Maybe she saw in me the parts of her that had to grow up too soon, the strength she had no choice but to carry. Maybe she was trying to teach me how to survive in a world that had shown her no mercy. Still, that understanding doesn't erase the weight I carried. It doesn't undo the ache of feeling more like the helper than the child. However, it did allow me to realize that what I had longed for most wasn't less responsibility—it was to be seen, to be nurtured, to just *be*, yet I can now hold both truths: *it was unfair*, and *I still became strong because of my experience.*

Grief has a way of bringing these old wounds to the surface. Losing her forced me to reflect not only on what she gave me, but also on what I needed and didn't receive. It made me see that healing isn't just about mourning the person we lost—it's also about healing the parts of ourselves that were shaped by them.

Today, I give that younger version of me permission to rest. I let her know that she did enough, that she *was* enough. I remind her that she doesn't have to be the strong one anymore.

My Precious Lessons

Understanding often comes with time—and compassion follows understanding.

For years, I carried resentment toward my mother for the way she raised me. I saw only the weight she placed on my shoulders, not the strength she was trying to build within me. I spent so many years being angry at her that I missed valuable moments I could have cherished. In that anger, I didn't realize how much time was slipping through my hands. Now I understand that love is always present, even in the broken places, and I hold those memories with tenderness instead of regret—using them as a reminder to choose grace, forgiveness, and presence while there is still time. It took losing my mother to realize that she wasn't being hard in order to break me—she was being hard in order to prepare me.

I now know that love doesn't always look gentle, and protection doesn't always come wrapped in tenderness. Sometimes love looks like survival—like doing what you can with what you have. I learned to see my mother as a woman first: flawed, human, and trying. And in that realization, forgiveness found me.

Gems Along The Way

The things that helped me heal during my time of grief that may also help you are:

- **Adjusting my expectations:** Healing began when I stopped expecting the past to change and started asking what it was trying to teach me.

- **Speaking my truth:** Allowing myself to tell the truth—that I was hurt, that I felt unseen, and that I longed for the kind of mother-daughter closeness I thought I missed out on. Speaking it out loud released its power over me.

- **Cultivating my peace:** Prayer kept me grounded. Journaling gave me a voice. Therapy brought me clarity. Together, they carried me through my healing journey. But most of all, giving grace—to my mother and to myself—gave me peace.

- **Holding both truths:** If you're struggling with the weight of a complicated relationship, try to hold both truths—that you were hurt and that they were human. Healing doesn't require choosing sides between love and pain; it's learning to carry both with gentleness.

Journal to Healing

Take a moment to sit with what you've read in this chapter. Reflect on your own journey with your mother, or the person who played an important role in your life. Let this be a space where your grief is allowed to exist—just as it is. In your journal, write your thoughts freely, openly, and honestly—without judgment, without pressure. There are no wrong answers here, only truth waiting to be realized.

1. How did your relationship with your mother or caregiver shape who you are today?

2. In what ways were you asked to be "the strong one" before you were ready?

3. What emotions do you still carry from your childhood that need acknowledgment?

4. What would forgiveness—for them or for yourself—look like today?

5. If you could speak to your younger self, what would you tell them about love, grace, and letting go?

- THREE -

Healing Through Her Story

A s I began doing the healing work to see my mother through new eyes, something within me began to shift. Understanding her story helped me start rewriting my own. I realized that healing wasn't just about forgiving her—it was also about nurturing the parts of me that still longed for her love and guidance. In the quiet spaces of reflection, I began to talk to God more, to search for strength beyond what I had carried all my life. Faith became the bridge between who I was and who I was becoming— the woman learning to mother herself, to trust her own heart, and to keep going even when the anchor was gone.

I began to reflect on the light my mother brought into my life—the way her voice was my grounding wire. She could soothe my soul with just a few words. It wasn't just what she said, but how she said it—with honesty, rawness, and that steady, unwavering look in her eyes that silently said, "I've got you—right, wrong, or indifferent." And she meant it. Every time.

In every pivotal moment of my life, my mother was there. She stood in the crowd, cheering as I walked across the stage for my high school diploma. She celebrated when I earned my college degree, and she encouraged me when I packed up my life to move to another state. She clapped for me when I landed my first corporate job, and she stood by my side when I gave birth to my daughter on January 3, 2011—the most sacred role I would ever take on.

But she wasn't just present in the good times. She was there in the storms too. Through the drama of broken relationships, through the crushing weight of being indicted on federal charges, through the heartbreak of being sentenced to more than a decade in prison. She even found ways to be present when I was separated from my daughter—those were my darkest days, and yet her voice, her prayers, and her faith carried me.

———————

February 22, 2011, is the day I was forced to leave my family behind. My daughter was just seven weeks old when a knock came at the door, followed by my arrest on a drug conspiracy indictment. At 28 years old, I walked out of my home in handcuffs, not knowing when—or if—I'd be able to hold my baby girl again.

My mother always reminded me during my incarceration that "we" were doing the time together—one day at a time. On the days when I felt like giving up, I would call her, and she never failed to pour life and strength back into me. She would tell me to hold on to that tiny mustard seed of faith, promising that if I didn't let go, I'd make it through another day stronger than I was the day before. She was right, every single time. I prayed my way through the night, and—just as the Scripture says—*joy always came in the morning* (Psalm 30:5).

Then, as if life had not already demanded enough of her strength, tragedy struck again—repeatedly—within just six years. While she was still carrying the weight of my absence and pouring encouragement into me during my darkest season, my mother was forced to face heartbreak after heartbreak of her own. Six months after my arrest, on July 13, 2011, my mother faced a mother's worst nightmare. She received the devastating news that her firstborn son—my younger brother—had been shot multiple times and killed near the trade school he once attended. He was only 22. She grieved the murder of her nephew, my first cousin, in 2014. She laid three of her sisters to rest, one in 2015 and two in 2016. And then came the unthinkable blow: finding her husband lifeless in the bathroom also in 2016. Through it all, she never returned to her addiction. Instead, she pressed forward, clinging tightly to her mustard seed of faith—small but mighty, steady enough to carry her through the storms.

Guilt weighed heavily on me. I wanted so badly to be by my mother's side as she grieved, to support her the way she had supported me. But instead, I was behind prison walls, feeling like a burden—even though she never once made me feel that way.

When I was around the age of 30, my mother began to open up to me in ways she never had before. Our conversations grew deeper, more honest, more tender. Slowly, our bond strengthened. I'll never forget the day she told me that, if anything good had come out of my imprisonment, it was that our relationship had grown closer than ever before. Through her openness and willingness to share her life story with me, I gained a newfound respect for her—one that redefined everything. I saw a woman who had survived unimaginable trials, who had faced her demons and still chose to fight. She became my warrior, my ideal, and my living example of resilience. Suddenly, the idealized image of Claire Huxtable didn't compare. My mother was greater—because she didn't live in a scripted world. She endured real struggles, real pain, and still rose above it all without giving up on herself or on life.

My Precious Lessons

Grief reshapes us in ways we never expect.

Losing my Nanny forced me to see the raw realities of life far too soon. Watching my mother's transformation—from battling addiction to standing firm in faith—taught me that resilience doesn't come from perfection, but from persistence. I also learned that relationships, even broken ones, can be rebuilt at any age through honesty, forgiveness, and grace.

Gems Along The Way

The things that helped me heal during my time of grief that may also help you are:

- **Faith as an anchor:** Even the smallest mustard seed of faith can keep you steady through storms.

- **Allowing perspective to shift:** When I stopped comparing my mother to who I thought she should be, I was able to see and appreciate the woman she truly was.

- **Honest conversations:** Deep, vulnerable talks helped heal wounds that silence only deepened.

- **Leaning into love, not guilt:** Even when I felt like a burden, my mother reminded me that love carries weight better than shame ever can.

Journal to Healing

Take a moment to sit with what you've read in this chapter and reflect on your own journey. Allow the truth to gently rise to the surface. Let this be a space where your grief is allowed to exist—just as it is. In your journal, write your thoughts freely, openly, and honestly—without judgment, without pressure. There are no wrong answers here, only truth waiting to be realized.

1. Reflect on your own relationships—especially the complicated ones. What unspoken expectations or comparisons might be preventing you from seeing someone as they really are?

2. Where have you seen resilience in your own family or in yourself?

3. What small "mustard seed" of faith (or hope) are you holding onto right now that keeps you moving forward?

- FOUR -

When Faith Had to Carry Me

The year 2019 began on a high note. My mother was finally in a good place—steadily finding her footing and learning to live again after so many losses. I was in my eighth year of incarceration in Lexington, Kentucky, holding on to faith and the hope of coming home soon. My daughter was eight years old, growing up faster than I could bear to imagine. Despite the challenges I had endured, by the grace of God, I was still standing—grateful to feel that the hardest part of my sentence was finally behind me.

The weekend of April 19 – 21, my mother, sister, and daughter came to visit me on their annual visit. Because the journey was over 10 hours away from home, I did not expect them to visit often. So, when I received a visit, it was always sacred to me, and this one was no different. We laughed until our stomachs hurt, snapped pictures to freeze the moments, and caught up on the pieces of life I couldn't touch from inside those walls. I noticed my mother's weight loss right away and told her how good she looked. She threw her head back with that big, beautiful smile of hers and said, "Y'all better hope you look this good when you get to my age." We all laughed, but deep down I held on to that image of her smile—it carried me through long nights and hard days. Visits like that gave me fuel, a boost of strength I needed to keep pushing through the time I still had left.

On Mother's Day, May 12, 2019, I did a video visit with my mother to wish her a Happy Mother's Day. To my surprise, she answered from a hospital bed. She had mentioned pain during some of our earlier phone calls, but I never imagined it had gotten serious enough to land her there. My sisters and I often teased her about being a hypochondriac—her go-to response for almost anything was, *"Go to the emergency room."* This time, though, it wasn't just one of her usual trips. I heard whispers in the background, but didn't think much of it. Then, my cousin took the phone and slipped into the bathroom. Her smile from seeing me went away, and her tone was different—serious, almost heavy—as she said, *"Cousin, I have to tell you something."*

I still didn't think it was anything extreme, so I responded calmly, *"Okay."*

That's when the words that changed everything came out: *"Your mom may have cancer."*

My mind instantly went to breast cancer. But before I could even form the question, she continued: *"Pancreatic cancer."*

I had no real idea of what that meant medically. I only knew from the sound of it that it had something to do with the pancreas—and somehow, just hearing the name made it feel even more frightening.

My cousin handed the phone back to my mom, and almost instantly, she reassured me in her steady voice that she was going to be alright.

32

With tears streaming down my face, I echoed her own words back to her, reminding her, *"WE are going to get through this together, one day at a time."*

When I hung up, I felt a flicker of hope rise within me. I knew my mom—she was a fighter through and through. Giving up was never in her spirit, and I believed with everything in me that she would do whatever it took to overcome this battle.

I immediately rushed to find a staff member, asking them to help me research pancreatic cancer. Within minutes, we pulled up the Pancreatic Cancer Action website, and the words on the screen nearly took my breath away. The statistics were devastating: the overall one-year survival rate was just 24.4%. Only 8 in 100 people lived five years or longer. And the ten-year survival rate was a mere 1%. 1 in 100. Reading those numbers felt like a punch to the stomach. I began piecing things together in my head, like my mother's sudden weight loss and constant complaints of pain. It was as if the hope I had been holding onto began to slip right through my hands.

About two weeks later, during another video visit with my mom and older sister, my mom confirmed what the doctor had told her—it was 90% certain to be stage-2 pancreatic cancer. Still, she held tightly to faith, praying on that 10% chance that it wasn't. While holding onto that hope, she began radiation on June 25, 2019. Her radiation team was called the "Green Team." She had so much support behind her that soon green became her color of strength. Family and friends wore it proudly as a sign of solidarity, standing with her through the fight. The first day of treatment was as rough as we expected. Between the chemo and radiation, her body was pushed to its limits.

Every treatment day, I made sure to call home. Most times, she was too drained to talk for long and would sleep the day away, but I just needed to hear her voice. Even in those short calls, I kept praying, believing her breakthrough was on the way.

On November 6, 2019, my mother completed her first round of radiation and proudly rang the bell. The treatments had shown signs of shrinkage, and for the first time in a long time, we ended the year feeling hopeful—holding on to the belief that brighter days were ahead.

Then came January 2020. I was now entering my ninth year of incarceration when the news of COVID-19 began spreading across the United States filled me with dread. I worried constantly about my mom, knowing how vulnerable she was with her weakened immune system. The world was shutting down, and all I could think about was whether my mother's strength would be enough to withstand not just cancer, but this new invisible threat.

On February 5, 2020, the prison went on lockdown to limit the spread of COVID-19 after positive cases were reported in the facility. My world caved in immediately. I was restricted to two phone calls a week, each only fifteen minutes long. I had been used to speaking with my mother daily, and the thought of losing her during this time—without being able to hear her voice—started to feel terrifyingly real. I made it a point to send her a letter every week, checking in, letting her know she was in my thoughts and prayers.

During these calls, my mother shared that her continued prayers were for:

- Her health to be restored.
- Justice for my brother's murder.
- And for me to make it home safely before God called her home.

Hearing her speak that prayer out loud made the fear I'd been trying to ignore suddenly real. It was a truth I wasn't ready to face—one my heart refused to accept.

Meanwhile, my mother's treatment plan progressed aggressively— radiation followed by chemotherapy—and the toll on her body was visible. I'll never forget the time I called her, and she was in the bathroom looking in the mirror, and she touched her hair, and it began falling out in clumps. She cried, and I reassured her that short hair looked amazing, and if anyone could pull it off, it was her. She gathered herself for the remainder of the conversation, but I knew that reality had finally settled in. In that moment, I felt helpless, knowing my mother needed me physically, and once again, I couldn't be there.

I held onto hope that a breakthrough would come, that somehow, I could get home earlier. My scheduled release was in 2023—three long years away—a seemingly impossible distance while my mother battled for her life.

COVID-19 continued to rage across the country, and positive cases inside the prison tripled. The Bureau of Prisons (BOP) was under growing pressure as lives hung in the balance. In response, they began releasing individuals under the Coronavirus Aid, Relief, and Economic Security (CARES) Act.

The CARES Act allowed certain incarcerated people to apply for compassionate release or home confinement—giving them the chance to either have their sentence reduced or serve the remainder at home on an ankle monitor. Compassionate release, however, was complicated and typically reserved for those with terminal illnesses or individuals whose loved ones—the primary caregivers of their children—were facing life-threatening conditions.

As my case manager, Mr. Williams, started having people sign paperwork for early release, I couldn't resist joking with him. Every time he walked by, I'd wave a pen and say, "I'm ready to sign my papers, Mr. Williams!" He'd just shake his head and remind me that I wasn't eligible because of how much time I still had left on my sentence.

Still, I kept it up. I even told him, half-serious and half just to get on his nerves, *"I don't know how or when, but I'm getting out of here before the year's over."* At the time, I didn't truly believe it—but something in me kept speaking it anyway.

On August 17, 2020, I submitted my motion for compassionate release because of my mother's illness. I knew it was a long shot—after all, I had filed over ten motions in the past, all denied—but it was a shot worth taking. I prepared myself for the disappointment.

On October 13, 2020, I received a response to my motion from the Assistant United States Attorney. He was totally against my early release. Tears filled my eyes as I read it; the discouragement was overwhelming. I felt hope slipping away. My mother reminded me, though, that we served a God who sits high and looks low, and that we did not have to fear man because God had the final say. Her words always gave me strength, but at that moment, the attorney's denial felt heavier.

December 14th, 2020, my mom was running late for a doctor appointment when she heard a knock at her door. It was a United States Probation Officer stating that he was told by the judge to come visit where I would stay if I were released. My mom asked if that meant I was coming home, and he stated NO, it was just protocol. She immediately emailed me, instructing me to call her. When I called home, she was screaming, shouting, and praising God in advance for answering her prayers. Even though it was a long shot, her faith allowed her to believe I was coming home.

December 16th, 2020, I was asked by a fellow Sister in Christ, Ms. Nancy, to read something at church. I asked her to give me the reading ahead of time to read it over, but she never did. I went to church and sat in the back of the room. Ms. Nancy began the Bible study by saying the topic was "A Compassionate Heart." Immediately, I began to shake my head. Nobody knew I was waiting for a response to my compassionate release, nor did they know the judge had requested that a probation officer visit my mom's apartment. I told myself that I was going to keep it to myself because I didn't want anyone's negative energy to sabotage my hopes. Ms. Nancy continued, she said, when God does something good for you, you are supposed to thank him first, then tell others of His good deed to give them hope (Psalm 77:12). I started shaking my head. Ms. Nancy asked me why I was shaking my head, and I began to laugh. I told her she was speaking directly to me. With hesitation and nervousness, I stood up and began to tell everyone what was going on. By the time I finished releasing everything, tears began to flow. It was a cry that came from the depths of my soul—both painful and freeing. My sisters in the church surrounded me, joining together in prayer. In that sacred moment, I felt God's presence fill the room, and I knew my breakthrough was on the way.

When I returned to my room and told my roommate everything that had transpired, she looked at me and said, *"We're going to claim your release date."* Together, we started looking at the calendar for the following week. It was the week of Christmas. We laughed and agreed that December 24th was too close to the holiday, so we boldly claimed **December 23, 2020, as my release date.**

The next morning, I walked into my case manager Mr. Williams's office with confidence. *"I'm going home on December 23rd,"* I told him, my voice steady with faith. He gave me a small smile and nodded, the kind of nod that said he'd heard similar declarations before. But this time, I knew deep in my spirit—it was already done.

December 22, 2020, I began my morning listening to The Steve Harvey Morning Show. Steve Harvey does this final segment where he gives closing remarks for the day. On this day he spoke about having an abundant life. He explained how we should talk and pray to God about EVERYTHING, praying without ceasing (1 Thessalonians 5:16). He continued saying, God wants us to just get through the day and free our minds. God wants us to relax and stop stressing and instead be on the lookout for what He is doing. Steve Harvey ended the segment with, *"Live your life in EXPECTATION!"* It was just what I needed to hear. I did not have to stress because God wanted me to relax while He worked everything out with my paperwork. I said a silent prayer and resumed my day.

Around 3:00 pm, I was in my room when I heard the secretary call my name. She asked me if I knew my mother's number by heart. I quickly responded yes, wondering what was wrong with my mom. She closed her office door and told me to call her. I cut her off and asked her why I needed to call her. My heart sank as I began to think the worst. She finished her sentence and said, *"Call her, because you were granted early release."* The judge approved your compassionate release motion, and you have to be off the premises by 7:00 pm. She continued with, *"You told Mr. Williams you were going to be home on December 23, 2020, and by the time your train gets you home, it will be December 23rd, 2020."* I instantly began crying.

The impossible became reality. I shook as I dialed my mom's number, and when she answered, I screamed, *"I am coming home!"* She screamed and called my older sister, who also screamed in disbelief.

I went to visit Mr. Williams before I left, and his final words to me were, *"It was your faith that got you home."* I smiled and thanked him for believing in me.

That day, after months of fear, prayers, and uncertainty, my prayers were answered. Hope was restored, and I could finally return home to my family.

My Precious Lessons

There is wisdom hidden inside the pain, the prayers, and the perseverance.

During this season, I learned that faith can override facts in ways that still leave me in awe. The doctors had statistics, the justice system had rules, and life had already shown me its harshest realities—yet God had a plan that stretched beyond every limitation. I discovered that hope can survive even in the darkest places, even behind prison walls, even while watching the strongest person I knew fight for her life. Love became a source of strength I didn't know I needed; my mother's belief in me and her unwavering faith reminded me that connection can outlive circumstance. And through it all, I realized that breakthrough often arrives at the moment we stop trying to control the outcome and instead, allow God to move freely. When we hold on to even the smallest seed of belief, miracles have room to unfold.

Gems Along the Way

The things that helped me heal during my time of grief that may also help you are:

- **Being Strong:** Leaning on the strength rooted in me, not the challenges standing before me.

- **Speaking Life Over My Circumstances:** Declaring what I believed God could do—even before I saw evidence—strengthened me from the inside out.

- **Staying Connected to My Mother:** Letters, calls, and shared prayers became emotional anchors that helped bridge the physical distance.

- **Allowing Myself to Break Down:** Giving myself permission to cry created space for release, healing, and emotional honesty.

- **Leaning on My Sisterhood:** Letting others pray with me and for me carried me when I didn't have strength of my own.

- **Surrendering Control to God:** Choosing trust over fear allowed peace to replace panic and opened doors I once believed were permanently closed.

- **Embracing Faith, Connection, and Vulnerability:** These practices together carried me through one of the hardest seasons of my life.

Journal to Healing

Take a moment to sit with what you've read in this chapter and reflect on your own journey. Allow the truth to gently rise to the surface. Let this be a space where your grief is allowed to exist—just as it is. In your journal, write your thoughts freely, openly, and honestly—without judgment, without pressure. There are no wrong answers here, only truth waiting to be realized.

1. Reflect on a moment when life shifted unexpectedly. What emotions surfaced? What fears or hopes came with that change?

2. Think about someone you love who has shown resilience. What did their strength teach you about your own?

3. Consider a situation that feels impossible right now. What small "mustard seed" of faith or hope are you holding onto?

4. Write about a time you tried to control the outcome. What changed when you loosened your grip or surrendered it to God?

5. Explore where your heart needs healing. What truth do you need to say out loud—even if only on the page?

6. Identify a statement of faith you want to declare today. What bold truth do you want to speak over your life?

- FIVE -

Transitioning Back Home

After 9 years and 10 months away, the day I had prayed for finally came. Walking out of those gates, I felt both the weight of the years I'd lost and the overwhelming relief of stepping back into freedom. Every breath felt new—like I was inhaling hope for the first time in a long time. But more than anything, I couldn't wait to see my mother.

Instead of taking the train home, my sister surprised me by booking a flight to Baltimore International Airport. I thought walking into an airport after so many years would feel overwhelming, but to my surprise, I blended right in. I retrieved my boarding pass, made it through the checkpoints, and took my seat in the waiting area—each step feeling surreal, like I was moving through someone else's life. I had dreamed of this moment over and over again. In my mind, I pictured myself running into my mother's arms, both of us crying tears of joy, picking up right where we left off. But when I finally saw her standing there in real life, reality hit me far harder than I ever expected.

My mother looked smaller—frailer—but still radiant in spirit. Her smile still carried warmth, her eyes still sparkled with strength. But behind that smile, I saw the quiet fatigue, the toll cancer had taken on her body. The woman who once seemed invincible, the one who had held our family together through every storm, was now fighting the hardest battle of her life.

When she saw me, she ran to me, picked me up off the ground, and spun me around. I could not believe that she had the strength to pick me up. It must have been her adrenaline taking over. Her whole face lit up. *"My baby's home,"* she whispered, her voice cracking as she pulled me into her arms. That hug—soft, trembling, and full of everything words couldn't express—was the healing I didn't know I still needed.

She continued to hold me tightly while my sisters, niece, and best friend also surrounded me with love. Then she burst out and said, *"We did that time, baby. We walked that time down, one day at a time."*

Walking out of the airport, I felt the truth settle on me: coming home wasn't going to erase the pain of what she had been fighting. Freedom was a blessing, yes—but it also meant facing reality without the distance of prison walls. I was finally home, yet I could feel that time was no longer on our side.

Every day that followed, I cherished the time I had with her like it was sacred. We laughed, reminisced, and sometimes just sat in silence. There was comfort in simply being near her again. I could feel how precious every moment was. My sisters had done so much for our mother during my absence, and now it was time for me to assist with her. The roles between my mom and me had changed. I was now the one encouraging her—I was the one making sure she took her medicine, helping her move around her apartment, cooking meals for her, even when she barely ate. Making sure she had her hot cup of tea daily. Watching her decline was devastating.

It's a helpless feeling to watch the strongest person you know—your anchor—grow weaker each day. Cancer had a way of stealing moments, energy, and sometimes hope. But what it could never steal was her spirit. She never complained, never allowed pity to take root. She still found ways to make us laugh, still encouraged me to keep going, to live, to stay strong no matter what came next.

On February 1, 2021—only 41 days after my release—my mother was admitted to the hospital. When I walked into her room, I immediately knew something was terribly wrong. She was delusional, unable to speak clearly, and had no awareness of what was happening around her. She recognized me, but whenever I asked her simple questions—"Are you okay?" "Do you need anything?" "Do you know where you are?"—she would only stare blankly or give a slight nod. There was no expression, no connection, no spark behind her eyes. It was as if the woman I knew was trapped somewhere I couldn't reach.

For two days, I sat by her side, watching her drift in and out of confusion, praying silently, trying not to let fear consume me. On the third day, something in my spirit told me to shift the atmosphere. I pulled out my phone and began playing gospel music—songs that had always lifted her spirit and steadied mine.

By the third song, *"I Can't Give Up Now"* by Mary Mary, something miraculous happened. Out of nowhere, my mother began singing—soft at first, then stronger with each word. I froze, stunned, and then tears began pouring down my face. The nurse stepped into the room, shocked to see her singing after days of unresponsiveness.

Every song that played afterward, she sang along as if she had never been disconnected at all. In that moment, the entire room felt charged with God's presence. I began praising and thanking Him right there at her bedside—because what I was witnessing wasn't just improvement. It was an intervention.

Little by little, she started returning to herself. Her awareness came back. Her eyes regained their focus. Her voice found its strength again. When she was fully alert, she had no memory of the previous days—no recollection of the confusion, the silence, or the blank stares.

The doctors examined her and ultimately concluded that she had suffered a severe episode of dehydration. But in my spirit, I knew it was deeper than that. I had watched her slip away and then witnessed God pull her back through the very songs that had carried us both through so many storms.

It was a moment I will never forget—a reminder that even when the mind fades and the body weakens, the soul still remembers who to call on.

Months later, my mother was having a particularly rough day. She was weak, tired, and barely able to hold herself up. She looked me straight in the eyes and asked softly, "Am I a burden to you?" Without hesitation, I told her she could *never* be a burden to me—just like she always told me I was never a burden to her. Then she said, *"Give me back the words I once gave you ... the ones that helped pull you through your darkest times."* In that moment, I reminded her that God had wrapped her in the same strength she once wrapped around me, and she didn't have to fear anything.

She squeezed my hand with what little strength she had left, and in that small gesture, I felt a lifetime of love pass between us. It was as if she was saying, *"Thank you ... I can rest now."*

The woman who had carried me through every storm—through childhood, through incarceration, through heartbreak—was now letting me carry her. And instead of fear, I felt a quiet honor settle in my spirit. I wasn't losing her; I was walking her gently toward peace. Every prayer she ever prayed for me, I now prayed over her. Every comforting word she once whispered to calm my trembling heart, I now offered back to her. It was a sacred exchange—love completing its circle.

There were days I'd walk into her room and find her whispering prayers, thanking God for another sunrise. Even when her body was failing, her faith never wavered. "I'm still here," she'd say, *"and while I'm here, I'm going to live."*

Her resilience reminded me of everything she had already overcome—the losses, the pain, the heartbreak—and yet she still chose joy. She still showed up for others. She still mothered, even while fighting for her own life.

Reuniting with her after so long was both a gift and a heartbreak. I got to love her in person again, to show up for her like she always showed up for me, to be the daughter she always believed I could be. But I also had to face the cruel reality that time wasn't on our side.

There were nights when I'd cry quietly after tucking her in, struggling as I wondered if I could continue as her caregiver. At times, I wanted to just be her daughter. I continually asked God for just one more day, one more smile, one more chance to tell her how much she meant to me. And somehow, God granted us many more of those days—each one filled with grace, laughter, and love.

Even as her body weakened, her spirit grew stronger. She became my reminder that even when life takes from you, it also gives—new perspectives, deeper love, and peace that surpasses understanding.

When I look back now, I see that those final months with her were a sacred exchange of strength. I thought I came home to care for her, but in truth, she was still caring for me—teaching me how to live, how to trust God, and how to love through the hardest moments.

My Precious Lessons

The spirit recognizes what the body forgets.

Even when her mind was confused and her body weak, the words of those songs reached a place in her that illness couldn't touch. It showed me that faith lives in the deepest parts of us—the parts that don't rely on memory, logic, or even physical strength. What God plants in the soul cannot be erased, not even by sickness. Watching my mother fight with grace reminded me that strength isn't about never breaking—it's about showing up every day with faith despite the pain. I learned that true strength isn't always loud—it's often quiet, gentle, and wrapped in love. I learned that the roles between mother and daughter can shift without warning, and when they do, love rises to meet the moment with a grace that feels almost sacred.

I discovered that caregiving is not a burden but a privilege, a chance to honor the very person who shaped your foundation. I learned that peace doesn't always look like understanding; sometimes it looks like acceptance, soft and slow. Most of all, I learned that love really does complete its circle—what is given out in one season often returns in another, fuller and deeper than before. Even in loss, I realized that love does not abandon us. It transforms, it carries, and it teaches us how to keep living with both strength and softness.

Gems Along The Way

The things that helped me heal during my time of grief that may also help you are:

- **Practice mindfulness:** Be present. Even quiet moments can be healing.
- **Be open:** Say what's in your heart—often.
- **Create memories:** Take pictures. Write memories down. You'll cherish them later.
- **Be in worship:** Pray together. It builds peace in the middle of pain.

Journal to Healing

Take a moment to sit with what you've read in this chapter and reflect on your own journey. Allow the truth to gently rise to the surface. Let this be a space where your grief is allowed to exist—just as it is. In your journal, write your thoughts freely, openly, and honestly—without judgment, without pressure. There are no wrong answers here, only truth waiting to be realized.

1. Think about someone in your life who taught you strength through adversity. Write about one lesson they left behind that you still carry with you today.

- SIX -

Love Day

By the end of 2021, my mother made the decision to stop
chemotherapy and transition fully into hospice care. Her body was
tired—tired of fighting, tired of being poked and prodded, tired of the
battle that had taken more from her than any of us wanted to admit out
loud. She didn't say it with sadness. She didn't say it with fear. She said it
with peace—quiet, steady, courageous peace.

She told us she wanted to focus on quality of life rather than the fight.
She accepted her fate with grace, a kind of grace that can only come from
a woman who has survived storms most people could never imagine. But
as she accepted it, the rest of us struggled. It was now time for me, my
siblings, the family, and everyone who loved her to accept it too—and that
was a transition none of us were ready for.

She believed she was preparing us to live without her, doing her best to
give us time to process what life would look like when she was no longer
physically here. But can you ever truly prepare someone to live without
their anchor? An anchor keeps the vessel steady, holding it in place so it

doesn't drift aimlessly in search of itself. Without it, you're left fighting the current, trying to find your way in waters you've never navigated alone.

One day, she looked at me with fear in her eyes and said, "I'm scared." It wasn't the kind of fear that comes from being sick—it was something deeper. She didn't elaborate, but I knew. I believe she was scared of what life would be like for us without her. She worried for her grandchildren, especially the ones she spoiled relentlessly. She worried about whether we'd know how to carry ourselves the way she taught us. She worried about whether we'd be okay.

February 2, 2022, my mother was transported to a hospice facility due to a decline in her health and increased pain.

February 11, 2022, she was released and sent home. A hospice nurse made a comment to the family that she had never witnessed anyone come to hospice in my mother's state and leave as responsive as my mother. We smiled and reassured her that our mother was a fighter

February 12, 2022, my mother was up and moving. She held her arms up and said, "I'm getting stronger!"

My mother began reaching out to people, telling them to come and visit her before it was too late, and while she was still able to hold a conversation with them. She had me call her friend Freda on the phone, and she told her, *"We buried a lot of people together, now it's time to bury me."* Freda was in denial as well and did not want to hear my mom speak of her death that way.

My mother began writing her eulogy and program with those she wanted to speak and sing. Her biggest request was for someone to play the trumpet in the town square at 12 noon. That was a long stretch but that was her personality, she had to be in control of her life down to her very last breath. She even had her hairdresser come to the house to cut and dye her hair.

February 15, 2022, my mother stopped eating and speaking completely.

February 21, 2022, the hospice nurse came and evaluated my mother and said that she had less than 48 hours to live.

February 22, 2022

I still remember how perfect that date looked on the calendar—2/22/22. People were calling it Love Day, talking about angel numbers, alignment, divine timing, harmony, balance, and connection.

And for me, it was also the anniversary of the day I was taken from my family and incarcerated—eleven years to the exact day.

I woke up that morning at 5 a.m., and my first thought was of my mother. Not a passing thought—an urgency. A pull. My partner and I had just moved into a house about 10 mins away from my mother's apartment. Something in my spirit said, "Go to her." I threw on shoes, grabbed my keys, and ran straight out of the house. I just had to get to her.

When I walked into her apartment, she was staring directly at the front door as if she had been waiting for me. She had a 24-hour caregiver, but that morning she didn't want the caregiver—she wanted one of her children.

She could no longer speak, but her eyes were loud. They told stories her mouth could no longer form.

She was drenched in sweat. My partner and I immediately cooled her down with a cold washcloth and changed her clothes. Her breathing was heavy and strained, so we gave her oxygen to help her rest. I played gospel music to soothe her spirit—music she loved, music that always calmed her.

For a moment, she looked peaceful, almost like she had drifted into a quiet place within herself.

Then she tapped me with her leg—desperate to get my attention. She wanted to tell me something. She had something important to say. I leaned in, trying to understand, but her body could no longer form the words. To this day, I wish I knew what she wanted to tell me. I wish I had understood. I wish I had said more. Held her longer. Looked deeper into her eyes. But regret is cruel like that—it shows up with a highlight reel of every "what if" and "if only."

After we felt she was settled, my partner and I left briefly to get breakfast. But as soon as I stepped outside, I felt a heaviness in the air—thick and almost unnatural. It was as if the atmosphere shifted, as if the universe knew something I didn't yet. My spirit grew unsettled, and I remember thinking, *"Something doesn't feel right."* I tried to brush it off, but the weight lingered, following me with every step. I didn't know it then, but my heart was already preparing for what my mind couldn't yet grasp.

About an hour after I left, our pastor and First Lady arrived. They prayed over my mother, gently telling her that she could rest now—that she had done her part, fought her fight, and could finally release the weight she'd been carrying.

Shortly after they left, my baby sister arrived for her daily routine of bathing our mother and checking on her.

Then my phone buzzed.

11:13 a.m.: *"I'm calling hospice. Mommy's breathing isn't good. It's like she is gasping for air."*

By 11:16 a.m., I sprinted back into the apartment.

She was still alive—barely—but present. Her eyes were moving around the room. My cousin and her friend stood on her right. My baby sister stood on her left.

My baby sister and I hadn't spoken in months due to a disagreement. But none of that mattered when I walked through that door. I pushed everything aside and ran straight to my baby sis. I wrapped my arms around her and told her I loved her.

And in the most divine moment I have ever experienced, my mother slowly turned her head toward us … looked right at us … and within sixty seconds of our reconciliation—she took her final breath.

People say sometimes a loved one will hold on until they get what their heart needs most. I never believed it—until that day. She waited until her daughters were united. That was her final act of love. Her last offering. Maybe that's what she had been trying to get my attention for earlier. She had always encouraged me to mend things with my sister—and in that moment, her unspoken request came full circle.

I wish I could explain the sound grief makes the first time it enters your body. It is not a scream or a cry. It is a rupture. A silent shattering deep within your chest. Something breaks, but you can't see it. You just feel the collapse.

I couldn't breathe.

I couldn't move.

I couldn't comprehend that the woman who loved me without conditions, who prayed for me through prison, who held my world together—was gone. On Love Day.

Some call that a coincidence; I don't.

I call it a divine signature.

My mother left this earth on a day made entirely of twos—symbolizing pairs, balance, connection, love. And that is exactly who she was. She gave love freely, consistently, unconditionally. She made everyone feel seen. She lived Love Day every day long before that day existed.

But even knowing that didn't stop the hurt.

The hours after her transition were a blur—phone calls, tears, silence, the need to be strong for everyone else while I was crumbling inside. I knew she was in a better place, I knew she was at peace, I knew she was suffering no more, but none of those words could reach the part of me that had shattered.

I wanted her.

One more hug.

One more "I love you."

One more moment of her calling my name the way only she could.

But loss is final like that. It leaves you with silence—heavy, suffocating silence.

Time moves differently when your heart is broken. Minutes stretch. Days blur. Nights swallow everything. And in that fog, you start questioning everything—your purpose, your strength, even your will to keep moving.

But somewhere in that darkness, something else began.

A tiny flicker.

A faint whisper.

A reminder:

Her love didn't die. It transformed.

And slowly—very slowly—I realized that the beginning of my greatest pain was also the beginning of my rebuilding.

Losing her felt like losing direction. Like someone cut the GPS in the middle of the trip. I didn't know which way was forward. I didn't know how to be "okay" without her nod of approval. Who was I without her? Could I make decisions on my own? Was I strong enough?

I didn't have those answers then. If I'm honest, I still don't have all of them. But I do know this: our bond didn't end the day she passed. It just changed form.

Now I carry her in different ways. In how I speak to my daughter. In how I wrap love around people. In how I slow down and listen. I hear her in my own voice sometimes—and that used to make me cry. But now, it makes me smile.

Because even though the world went quiet, her love didn't because of the bond we shared.

There is no way to brace yourself from losing your mother. People try to prepare you. They tell you what to expect. They explain the stages of grief, the process, the signs. But when it actually happens, it hits you in a place no one can describe. One moment, she was here. The next, she wasn't. And I was not ready.

My Precious Lessons

I've learned that you can never truly prepare for losing your mother—but you can carry her with you. I learned that love doesn't end with death; it changes form. I learned that grief will strip you down, but it will also show you what you're made of. And I learned that anchors don't disappear—they become internal. The silence can feel unbearable at first, but it is often where the most honest healing begins. I learned that missing her doesn't mean I'm weak, and sitting in the quiet doesn't mean I'm stuck. It means I'm listening.

I also learned that my mother's absence didn't take her wisdom with it. Her voice lives on in how I think, how I love, and how I choose to move through the world. The quiet taught me that I am capable of standing on my own, even when I don't feel strong. And most importantly, I learned that silence is not empty—it holds memory, connection, and love in a different form.

Gems Along The Way

The things that helped me heal during my time of grief that may also help you are:

- **Releasing judgement:** Allowing myself to feel everything without judgment helped me most. Leaning into faith when nothing made sense. Letting love surround me, even when I felt undeserving.

Remembering her voice. Talking to her out loud. Trusting that rest was not a weakness. And believing—slowly—that healing didn't mean losing her. I stopped trying to fill every silent moment and allowed myself to sit with it. I lit candles, wrote letters to my mother, and spoke to her spirit when the ache felt too heavy. Journaling helped me release what I couldn't say out loud.

- **Faith also steadied me in the quiet:** It reminded me that even when I felt alone, I was still being held. Asking myself what my mother would want for me helped guide my choices and gave me permission to live fully again. Over time, I learned that the quiet didn't mean I had lost her—it meant our connection had changed.

Journal to Healing

Take a moment to sit with what you've read in this chapter and reflect on your own journey. Allow the truth to gently rise to the surface. Let this be a space where your grief is allowed to exist—just as it is. In your journal, write your thoughts freely, openly, and honestly—without judgment, without pressure. There are no wrong answers here, only truth waiting to be realized.

1. How does silence feel to you since your loss?

2. When does it show up the most?

3. What memories surface when things are quiet?

4. Do you try to avoid the silence, or have you allowed yourself to sit with it?

5. What might help you create safety and comfort for yourself in quiet moments?

- SEVEN -

When Grief Is Loud

G rief isn't always quiet.
Sometimes, it screams.

It screams in the middle of the night when the world is asleep, but your heart refuses to rest. It screams when you reach for your phone out of habit—to call her, to hear her voice—only to remember there's no one on the other end. It screams in the shower, in the car, in the grocery store aisle when you pass something she used to love, and the memory hits you without warning.

No one warned me how loud grief could be.

The days after my mother's passing felt unreal, like I was moving through someone else's life. People came. They hugged me tightly. They brought food. They offered words they thought would help.

"She's in a better place."

"Be strong."

"Time heals all wounds."

"She wouldn't want you to cry."

"She is with God.

Maybe they were right. I knew they meant well, but none of those words softened the silence that had taken up residence inside my soul. None of them filled the space she left behind. None of them brought her back.

What they don't tell you about grief is that it doesn't stay contained to one moment or one memory—it spreads. It shows up everywhere. In the clothes I couldn't bring myself to touch. In a familiar scent lingering as someone passed by. In videos of her dancing, laughing, and fully alive. In the voicemail I played over and over just to hear her say, *"I love you."*

Grief didn't arrive gently. It barged in—uninvited, unapologetic, with no intention of leaving. And I had no idea how to live with it.

I tried to stay busy. I tried to be present for my daughter. I tried to pray, sleep, and function. On the outside, life kept moving. On the inside, I was drowning quietly in a sea of memories.

In the days after her death, I couldn't eat. At night, I cried until my chest hurt. And the guilt—that was the loudest voice of all. Guilt for the things I didn't say. Guilt for wondering if I could have done more. Guilt for laughing one day and realizing hours had passed without thinking about her. Guilt for breathing when she no longer could.

Grief is messy. It doesn't follow a schedule. Some days I was okay—or at least convincing myself I was. Other days, I couldn't get out of bed. There were no rules. No timeline. No clear path forward.

Three months after she passed, I walked into a room full of people and felt completely alone. My body was there, smiling, responding—but my soul was somewhere else. Curled up beside her absence, whispering, *"How do I go on without you?"*

And then came the voices in my own mind:

You need to pull it together.

You're a mother—your daughter needs you.

You're strong. You've survived worse.

But this was different. I wasn't just grieving a death. I was grieving my anchor. My compass. My safe place. The person who knew me before I spoke, who steadied me when I drifted, who loved me without conditions.

Still, even in the noise, something softer began to surface. A memory. A lesson. Her voice—steady and familiar—whispering, *"You're going to be okay, baby. Just take it one day at a time."*

And so, I did.

Some days, the loudness still wins. A song will play. A scent will pass me by. A memory will rise, and I'll crumble all over again. But more often now, I'm learning how to sit with the grief without letting it swallow me whole. I'm learning that crying doesn't make me weak, and laughing doesn't mean I've forgotten her.

I'm learning that grief is just love with nowhere to go.

And maybe—just maybe—it's okay to let it be loud sometimes.

My Precious Lessons

I learned that grief doesn't follow rules, timelines, or expectations—and trying to control it only makes it louder. I learned that strength doesn't mean silence, and breaking down doesn't mean I'm falling apart. It means I'm human. I learned that grief can coexist with joy, laughter, and even peace, without diminishing the love I carry for my mother. Most of all, I learned that grief is not something to "get over." It's something to learn how to live with—slowly, gently, and truthfully.

I also learned that when grief is loud, it's often asking to be acknowledged, not avoided. When I stopped fighting it and allowed myself to listen, it became less overwhelming. Grief didn't disappear—but it softened when I gave it space.

Gems Along The Way

- **Allowing grief to speak instead of trying to quiet it:** I stopped judging my tears and let them come when they needed to. I gave myself permission to feel without explaining myself to anyone. Faith became a steady place for me when my emotions felt out of control—prayer helped me release what I couldn't carry alone.

- **Staying connected to my mother's memory:** I played her voicemails, talked about her openly, and allowed myself to remember her fully—not just in pain, but in love. I learned that grounding myself in small, simple moments—breathing deeply, sitting still, naming what I was feeling—helped bring the volume down when grief felt too loud.

- **Self-love and care:** Rest helped. Honesty helped. Letting go of guilt helped. And reminding myself that grief is love—not weakness—helped me begin to heal.

Journal to Healing

Take a moment to sit with what you've read in this chapter and reflect on your own journey. Allow the truth to gently rise to the surface. Let this be a space where your grief is allowed to exist—just as it is. In your journal, write your thoughts freely, openly, and honestly—without judgment, without pressure. There are no wrong answers here, only truth waiting to be realized.

1. When does grief feel the loudest for you?

2. What triggers or moments make it rise unexpectedly?

3. How do you usually respond when grief shows up—do you fight it, ignore it, or listen to it?

4. What might change if you allowed grief to speak without judgment?

5. What brings you even a small sense of grounding when emotions feel overwhelming?

- EIGHT -

Living in the Silence

After the first month of the noise came the quiet. Once the phone calls slowed down ...

Once the flowers wilt ...

Once the people got back to their lives ...

There's just silence.

It's a silence you don't prepare for. It's the kind that creeps in at 2 a.m. when the tears don't come, but the ache does. It's not dramatic. It doesn't scream like those early days. It just *is*—constant, cold, and present.

I remember walking into her room one afternoon. The bed was made just the way she used to do it—tight corners, smooth comforter, pillows fluffed just right. Her scent still lingered in the fabric. I sat down on the edge and stared at the place where she used to lie.

And it hit me: she wasn't coming back.

No phone call. No hug. No long talks in the kitchen about everything and nothing. I sat in that silence for what felt like hours, afraid to move. Afraid to disturb the air that still felt like her.

That's the part no one tells you—how grief lives in the quiet moments. When you go to cook and reach for her recipe. When you open a drawer and find her handwriting on a note. When you see something funny and instinctively think, *Ma would've cracked up at that.*

But she's not there. And the silence reminds you.

Sometimes I'd talk out loud to her, just to break it.

"Ma, I need you."

"Did I make the right choice today?"

"I miss you so much."

And every time, the silence would answer back—empty but sacred.

That silence forced me to confront myself. Without her voice guiding me, I had to start listening to my own. And that was terrifying. Because my voice had been shaped by hers. My wisdom mirrored hers. My softness was a reflection of hers.

So I started asking myself the question that changed everything:

What would Mommy want for me now?

Would she want me curled up in bed, numb and hollow?

Would she want me drowning in guilt?

Or would she want me to carry her light?

She would want me to *live*. Not just exist. Not just survive. She'd want me to stand tall—even broken—and move forward, even if slowly. She didn't raise me to fall apart and stay there. She raised me to rise, even when it hurt. I can still hear her voice saying, *"Fall in line, Girl Scout,"* and I would chuckle. That line was her go-to phrase whenever I felt like giving up. It came from my favorite movie, *"The Five Heartbeats."* Other times to make me laugh, she'd break into the gospel song *"I Won't Give Up Now"* by Mary Mary. By the time she finished, I'd be laughing so hard I'd forget why I was discouraged in the first place. She was able to comfort me face-to-face or through a telephone conversation miles away. She always knew the right words to say at the right time, whether you wanted to hear them or not.

So, I started finding meaning in the quiet. I lit candles and spoke to her spirit. I journaled. I let the silence become sacred. Not empty—but filled with her presence in a new form.

Some days, I still feel the quiet pressing on me like a weight. But now, I know she's in that quiet too. She's there when I cry. She's there when I laugh. She's there in the way I care for others, the way I show up for my daughter, the way I soften my voice when someone needs comfort.

The silence hasn't gone away. But I'm no longer afraid of it.

Because sometimes, silence is where love echoes the loudest.

My Precious Lessons

I learned that grief doesn't end when the noise fades—it simply changes its voice. The quiet can feel overwhelming at first, but it is often where the deepest healing begins. I learned that silence doesn't mean abandonment; it means invitation—an invitation to listen, to remember, and to grow.

I also learned that my mother's presence didn't disappear when her voice did. It transformed. Her guidance still lives in my decisions, my compassion, and the way I carry myself through the world. Living in the silence taught me that I am capable—even when I don't feel strong.

Gems Along The Way

The things that helped me heal during my time of grief that may also help you are:

- **Embrace the stillness:** Stop running from the quiet and instead make peace with it. Rather than filling every silent moment or avoiding it altogether, I began allowing the quiet to exist without fear. I learned that the silence wasn't there to harm me—it was there to teach me how to sit with my feelings and listen to what my heart needed.

- **Surround yourself with your community:** I also surrounded myself with my mother's close friends—people who knew her, loved her, and carried pieces of her spirit. Being in their presence grounded me when the silence felt too heavy to hold on my own. Through shared memories, laughter, tears, and familiar stories, the quiet softened. In those moments, I didn't feel so alone. I felt connected—to her, to community, and to the love that still surrounded me.

- **Hold on to faith:** Faith steadied me when my emotions felt unanchored. It reminded me that I wasn't truly alone, even when it felt that way. Asking myself what my mother would want for me helped guide my steps forward and gave me permission to live fully again.

- **Be patient:** Over time, I learned that the quiet wasn't taking something from me—it was giving me space to become who I needed to be next.

Journal to Healing

Take a moment to sit with what you've read in this chapter and reflect on your own journey. Allow the truth to gently rise to the surface. Let this be a space where your grief is allowed to exist—just as it is. In your journal, write your thoughts freely, openly, and honestly—without judgment, without pressure. There are no wrong answers here, only truth waiting to be realized.

1. How does silence feel for you since your loss?

2. When do you notice it the most?

3. What memories surface when things are quiet?

4. Do you try to fill the silence, avoid it, or sit with it?

5. What small ritual could help you feel supported during quiet moments?

- NINE -

Support Systems and Letdowns

G rief has a way of showing you who people really are.
There's a saying that when you lose someone, you also lose a few more people along the way. I never fully understood that—until I did.

In those first few days after my mom passed, people showed up. The calls came in. My inbox was full of *"I'm here if you need anything."* And for a while, I believed they meant it. But grief has a timeline most folks won't follow. People return to their routines, and you're still trying to remember how to breathe.

There were people I thought would be right beside me through it all—people who had known her, who had said they loved me. But slowly, they faded. The texts slowed. The check-ins stopped. The silence around me started to sound different—not just grief, but abandonment.

I was not angry. I was disappointed. A friend once told me at the beginning of my prison sentence, *"Expect nothing and appreciate everything."* At first, I didn't understand the depth of those words, but over time I realized how true they were. Holding on to expectations—of people, of outcomes, of how life *should* look—only left me disappointed and hurting. Letting go of those expectations became a form of protection and, eventually, a pathway to peace.

Now, I understand that not everyone knows how to show up for grief. Some people get uncomfortable around pain. Others think time should've "healed" me by now. Some just didn't know what to say, so they said nothing. Still, it hurt. But here's the part that surprised me: some people showed up who I never expected.

The quiet friend who just sat next to me and let me cry. The neighbor who brought food—not just once, but weeks later when she knew the loneliness had set in. The friend who didn't ask me how I was doing (because she knew the answer), but asked, *"Did you eat today?"* and *"Want to take a walk?"* The kind of presence that didn't ask anything of me—just offered love, in its most human form.

Then there was my daughter.

She grieved in her own way—trying to be strong, trying to be brave, apologizing for crying. I saw my 10-year-old self in her when I lost my Nanny. I knew that sadness in her eyes all too well. And even though I was shattered, I knew I had to keep going for her. She needed to know it was okay to cry. Okay to fall apart sometimes. Okay to need help. I wanted to model resilience, but also honesty. Because pretending doesn't heal anything—it just delays it.

I also leaned on God.

Not always gracefully. Sometimes I cried and asked *"Why would You take her from me? Why now?"* I felt abandoned by Heaven and lost in my faith. But even in those angry prayers, I knew God could handle my honesty. Slowly, I found comfort in little things—a verse, a song, a breeze that felt like her hand on my shoulder. Those quiet touches reminded me I wasn't alone.

Support during grief doesn't always come how you expect it. It might not be the people you thought. It might not be the words you were hoping for. But if you open your heart, you'll see the love still shows up.

It might be through a partner.

A child.

A friend.

A stranger.

A memory.

Or a prayer.

And while grief revealed a few letdowns, it also revealed the real ones—the ones who didn't need to be perfect, just present.

I hold deep gratitude for them. For their patience. For their compassion. For their quiet presence in my chaos.

Because in grief, it's not about fixing.

It's about *being*.

And those who stayed? They helped me remember I didn't have to heal alone.

My Precious Lessons

I learned that support doesn't always look the way we expect it to. Some people fall away not because they don't care, but because they don't know how to sit with pain. I learned that holding on tight to expectations can deepen disappointment, while releasing them creates space for peace.

I also learned that the people who truly matter in grief are the ones who stay present—without trying to fix, rush, or minimize the pain. Grief clarified who was safe, who was genuine, and who was capable of holding space for my truth.

Gems Along The Way

The things that helped me heal during my time of grief that may also help you are:

- **Release and appreciate:** Releasing expectations and appreciating the support that showed up—however it came created so much peace. I allowed myself to lean into the people who were consistent, quiet, and sincere.

- **Strength in faith:** I also found strength in faith, even when my prayers were messy and filled with questions. Letting myself be honest with God created room for healing. Watching my daughter grieve reminded me that vulnerability is not weakness—it's how we survive together.

- **Meaningful relationships:** Most of all, I learned that I didn't need a large crowd. I needed real presence.

Journal to Healing

Take a moment to sit with what you've read in this chapter and reflect on your own journey. Allow the truth to gently rise to the surface. Let this be a space where your grief is allowed to exist—just as it is. In your journal, write your thoughts freely, openly, and honestly—without judgment, without pressure. There are no wrong answers here, only truth waiting to be realized.

1. Who showed up for you during your grief?

2. How did their presence help—even in small ways?

3. Were there people you expected support from who didn't show up? How did that affect you?

4. What expectations might you need to release to protect your peace?

5. Who feels safe for you to lean on now?

TEN

The Unspoken Weight of Being the Strong One

B eing strong comes at a cost. People looked at me and saw strength. I made sure the bills were paid.

I checked on everybody else.

I kept moving.

I didn't break.

I survived, I guess.

I was the one who always seemed to bounce back.

But what they don't see about the strong one happens when the door closes.

What it feels like to collapse onto the bathroom floor because you didn't want your daughter to see you cry. What it feels like to scream into a pillow because the pain has nowhere else to go. What it feels like to have to be the "strong one" while feeling completely empty inside.

I had breakdowns that came without warning—anxiety attacks, gut-wrenching cries that felt like they would never end. I leaned heavily on my partner. In those moments, my partner didn't always know what to do. She wanted so badly to help me heal, but no one could fix a heart that shattered like mine. All she could do was hold me, whisper prayers over me, and stay by my side until I drifted off to sleep.

It's important to have someone you can be completely vulnerable with—because walking through grief alone is terrifying. Your mind and body will experience things you never knew they could. The emotional weight is unpredictable. Some days, it knocks you off your feet.

I tried to outrun my reality by staying busy, filling every minute to avoid facing the truth. But avoidance only delayed the pain—it didn't erase it. It buried it. And pain that's buried too long always finds its way back to the surface.

But surviving is not the same as healing.

There were days I wished someone would look me in the eye and say, *"You don't have to be strong today. Let me hold you."* Days when I wanted to whisper, *"I'm not okay,"* without fear that everything around me would fall apart.

Being the strong one is lonely. People assume you're fine. They assume you've got it under control. They don't ask questions. They don't notice when the smile is forced or the exhaustion sits heavy in your eyes. They lean on you, unaware that you're standing on cracked ground.

And after a while, you start believing the lie—that your worth is tied to how well you carry everything.

But here's the truth I've learned: strength does not require silence.

It's strong to admit you're hurting.

It's strong to ask for help.

It's strong to say no.

It's strong to cry.

It's strong to sit still and feel.

It's strong to say, *"Today, I don't have it in me."*

My strength didn't die when my mother did—but it changed. I began redefining it. Not as the woman who pretends to be okay, but as the woman who gives herself grace. The woman who lets others in. The woman who is healing out loud.

Two years later, when my heart was finally ready, I reached out for help. I began therapy and allowed myself to walk—slowly and intentionally— through the long, uncomfortable process of healing. Therapy didn't erase the pain, but it helped me breathe again, one layer at a time. As I sat in those sessions, I couldn't help but think about how I had suppressed the grief of losing my Nanny more than 29 years earlier. As I previously stated, in my family, therapy wasn't something we discussed or embraced. Like many Black families, we carried the belief that we should be strong, pray about it, and keep moving forward—never pausing long enough to tend to our wounds.

Therapy revealed how much unhealed grief I had been carrying since my Nanny's passing. Survival had been my only lesson. I learned how to keep going even when my world was falling apart, but no one ever taught me how to truly grieve. So, when my mother passed away, all those buried emotions from 1993 when Nanny passed away came crashing back over me like a tidal wave. Everything I had pushed down and "handled" as a child rose to the surface with a force I couldn't ignore.

This time, I chose differently. I chose vulnerability—a foreign, uncomfortable, almost frightening place for someone who had spent her whole life being told to be strong. I chose a new path, one that required me to stop pretending I was okay and finally confront the wounds I had spent decades avoiding. I chose to heal, not by suppressing the pain or powering through it, but by sitting with it, acknowledging it, and giving myself permission to feel every bit of what I had survived. Healing became a conscious decision—an everyday choice to break the cycles that shaped me and make room for a version of myself I had never met but desperately needed to become.

That's the weight of grief no one talks about.

When my mom passed, I didn't just lose my mother—I lost my safe space. She was the one who could sense when something was wrong before I ever said a word. She read my silence, my sighs, my pauses. She knew me in a way no one else ever has or ever will. And then, in a blink of an eye, without her, I suddenly became her—the person everyone called, the one people turned to when life got heavy, the place where others came to unload.

It happened so quietly I didn't even see the shift at first. One moment I was grieving, and the next, I was holding everyone else together. Even in my own brokenness, I tried to carry the weight of everyone's emotions because that's what the "strong one" does, right? The strong one shows up. The strong one listens. The strong one makes space for others even when there's none left inside themselves.

But no one tells you that being the strong one becomes even harder when the person who used to strengthen *you* is gone.

The weight of becoming everyone's anchor started revealing cracks I didn't even know were there. Every phone call, every visit, every moment someone leaned on me felt heavier than the last. I wanted to show up the way my mother always had, but my heart was running on empty. I was grieving and giving at the same time—pouring from a well that hadn't been refilled since the day she took her last breath.

That's when the truth that my mother never got to teach me directly hit me: even the strong one needs somewhere to fall. Even the person who holds everyone else together needs a place to lay their own burdens down. Strength without rest isn't strength—it's survival. And survival without vulnerability becomes suffocation.

But unlearning that pattern was hard. For years, I believed that asking for help made me weak. That showing emotion made me feel needy. That taking time for myself was selfish. Grief has a way of stripping you down to the truth, and the truth was simple: I needed help. I needed rest. I needed permission to not be okay.

Little by little, I began to soften. I let people pour into me instead of always being the one pouring out. I learned that boundaries weren't walls meant to keep people away—they were protection meant to keep me whole. They were an act of love toward myself, a way of honoring my own capacity.

I also found myself rethinking what my mother's strength really was. It wasn't in doing everything for everyone—it was in her faith, her resilience, her ability to rise after every storm she survived. If I truly wanted to honor her, I had to stop trying to replace her. I wasn't meant to fill her shoes—I was meant to walk in my own, using the foundation she gave me.

Grief taught me that strength and softness can coexist. That it's okay to be held. Healing began the moment I stopped trying to be everything for everyone, and finally allowed myself to be honest about my own pain.

Being the strong one almost broke me. Now, I'm learning to simply be human. I still carry a lot, but I no longer carry it alone.

So many people leaned on my mother when their world was falling apart. She was the fixer, the comforter, the steady one. But I remember her asking me once, *"Who does the strong lean on?"* That question stayed with me. Echoed through my grief. And even now, the only answer that makes sense is this:

God.

He was her source.

And now, in my most fragile moments, He has become mine.

My Precious Lessons

I've learned that strength is not about how much you can carry—it's about knowing when to set the weight down. I learned that being the strong one doesn't mean being unbreakable, and it certainly doesn't mean being silent. Strength that never rests eventually becomes exhaustion, not resilience.

I also learned that grief exposes patterns we didn't realize we were living in. For me, it revealed how deeply I equated worth with usefulness, and love with self-sacrifice. Losing my mother forced me to confront the truth that I had learned how to survive—but not how to receive.

Most importantly, I learned that I don't dishonor my mother by softening. I honor her by living fully, by choosing healing, and by allowing myself the same compassion she always gave so freely to others.

Gems Along The Way

The things that helped me heal during my time of grief that may also help you are:

- **Honesty:** Finally, giving myself permission to stop performing strength and start practicing honesty. Therapy gave me a space where I didn't have to be okay, where I could unpack grief layer by layer without judgment. It helped me understand that healing doesn't mean forgetting—it means integrating what you've lost into who you are becoming.

- **Allowing:** Leaning on safe people also helped—those who didn't need me to explain myself or show up perfectly. I learned to let others support me instead of always being the support. Creating boundaries helped protect my energy and reminded me that rest is not selfish—it's necessary.

- **Belief:** Faith became my foundation when my own strength ran out. I learned that I didn't have to carry everything alone, and that surrendering to God wasn't giving up—it was being held.

Journal to Healing

Take a moment to sit with what you've read in this chapter and reflect on your own journey. Allow the truth to gently rise to the surface. Let this be a space where your grief is allowed to exist—just as it is. In your journal, write your thoughts freely, openly, and honestly—without judgment, without pressure. There are no wrong answers here, only truth waiting to be realized.

1. Are you considered the "strong one" in your family or circle?

2. How has that role shaped the way you grieve?

3. Where do you feel pressure to keep it together, even when you're hurting?

4. What would it look like to let yourself soften—just a little?

5. Who or what feels safe enough for you to lean on right now?

ELEVEN

Rebuilding Through Routine

After the chaos, the stillness comes.

Grief is wild in the beginning—loud, messy, unpredictable. But eventually, it settles into the background of your life. Not because it's gone, but because your body gets tired of being in survival mode.

I remember waking up one morning—about two years after my mother passed—and realizing that I couldn't clearly recall the entire year that followed her death. Whole moments were missing, conversations blurred, days blended together. I had been moving, but not living. Functioning, but not feeling. I was just … existing.

I still don't know what shifted in me that morning, but something did. I realized I needed to find a rhythm again—not for appearances, not to keep up with the world, but for my own sanity. I had to start choosing myself in a way I hadn't done since she took her last breath.

I was in a depression and didn't even recognize it. Looking back, the signs were all there—I continually called off from work, I stopped engaging, stopped caring about the things that once brought me joy. Whole days slipped by where I barely moved from the bed. I wasn't sleeping to rest; I was sleeping to escape. I thought I was just "tired," but the truth was, I was sinking.

Thank God for my partner. In a season when I could barely hold myself together, she became the steady ground beneath me. She checked on me when I withdrew, made sure I ate, kept the house running, and handled the things I didn't have the strength to face. On mornings when simply opening my eyes felt impossible, she sat beside me without judgment. When I couldn't get out of bed, she didn't push—she supported me. She carried what I couldn't until I was strong enough to carry again.

I didn't have the language for depression then. I only knew I wasn't myself. And without my partner, I genuinely don't know how far I would've fallen. Depression crept in slowly, disguised as exhaustion, irritability, and numbness. I told myself I was just overwhelmed … just adjusting … just going through a rough patch. But the truth was, I had stopped living the day my mother took her last breath, and I never noticed how far I had drifted.

Everything felt unfamiliar without her. I used to talk to my mother two or three times a day—so much that she and my stepdad jokingly nicknamed me "Stalk," short for stalker. After she passed, every time my phone rang, I found myself wishing it was her. My routines fell apart. No self-care. No making the bed. No cooking. Even doing laundry felt impossible. The house felt heavy, especially in the quiet moments after my daughter left for school. Nothing felt like my life anymore—just an empty version of it that I was trying to move through. But deep down, I knew I couldn't stay in that funk forever.

Grief had stripped me bare, but healing began as soon as I stopped pretending that I was fine. I learned that you don't climb out of depression in one big leap—you crawl, you inch, you lift yourself out piece by piece.

So, I started with the small things.

I got up and made the bed.

I opened the blinds and let the light in.

I made myself tea—even when I didn't really want it due to it being my mother's morning drink.

I sat for five minutes and just *breathed.*

That's where healing began. Not in some big breakthrough. Not in a therapy session or a spiritual epiphany. Little by little, I started pulling myself back together. Not quickly. Not perfectly. But intentionally. It began in the routines. The repetition. The grounding.

I started writing again. Not whole chapters. Just a few words. A thought. A feeling. A memory. It helped me feel connected to her—like I was still talking to her, still keeping a part of her alive. Some days, I wrote letters to her. Other days, I just scribbled things like *"I miss you"* over and over again until the tears came.

I also started walking. Sometimes with music. Sometimes in silence. Just moving. Moving helped me feel alive again. Helped me process. Helped me release.

I started therapy to learn boundaries. By setting boundaries, it allowed me to protect my peace, honor my needs, and stop pouring from an empty cup. It wasn't easy at first—saying "no" felt uncomfortable, even selfish—

but over time, I realized boundaries weren't walls to shut people out; they were guardrails to keep me from losing myself.

Slowly, I added other pieces back into my routine. Cooking meals. Calling friends. Setting goals. Creating space for laughter. Not because I was "over" anything, but because I realized I deserved to live even while I grieved.

That was a turning point for me—realizing that joy and grief could exist in the same room.

Some days, the grief still won. I'd call off work, I'd cancel plans. I'd cry for hours. I'd shut down. But I gave myself permission for that too. Because healing isn't linear. It's not neat. It doesn't arrive with a clear ending. I need you to tell yourself … *I give myself permission to feel whatever emotions arrive today, and I remind myself that it's okay to simply be.*

But those routines—those ordinary, steady rhythms—they saved me.

They reminded me that life was still here. That I was still here. And that even in loss, I could begin again.

Brick by brick, breath by breath, routine by routine.

And that's what my mother would've wanted—not for me to "move on," *but to move forward.*

With intention.

With softness.

With her still with me—just in a different way.

My Precious Lessons

I learned that grief doesn't always need a breakthrough—it often needs structure. Routine gave me something solid to hold onto when everything else felt uncertain. I learned that depression can be quiet and slow, disguising itself as exhaustion or withdrawal, and that noticing it is the first step toward healing.

I also learned that rebuilding doesn't mean forgetting. It means choosing to live again while carrying love with you. Healing didn't erase my grief—it taught me how to coexist with it.

Gems Along The Way

The things that helped me heal during my time of grief that may also help you are:

- **Start small and stay consistent:** Simple routines—making the bed, opening the blinds, taking a walk—helped ground me when my emotions felt overwhelming. Writing gave me a place to release what I couldn't say out loud. Movement helped me reconnect with my body.

- **Seek support:** Therapy helped me name what I was experiencing. Boundaries helped me protect my energy. And allowing myself grace—on good days and hard ones—made the process sustainable.

- **Small steps:** Healing didn't come from doing everything at once. It came from doing one small thing, again and again.

Journal to Healing

Take a moment to sit with what you've read in this chapter and reflect on your own journey. Allow the truth to gently rise to the surface. Let this be a space where your grief is allowed to exist—just as it is. In your journal, write your thoughts freely, openly, and honestly—without judgment, without pressure. There are no wrong answers here, only truth waiting to be realized.

1. What routines have fallen away since your loss?

2. What is one small habit you could reintroduce into your day?

3. How does your body feel when you imagine creating a gentle rhythm again?

4. What helps you feel grounded, even for a few minutes?

5. What would it look like to give yourself permission to move forward slowly?

- TWELVE -

The Guilt of Moving On

I come from a family that knows how to laugh through pain. Humor has always been our bandage—covering wounds we never learned how to speak about. I mastered the art of smiling even when my heart was breaking, using my laughter as a shield to hide the heaviness inside me.

But after my mother passed, even that coping mechanism disappeared. My smile felt foreign. Forced. Heavy. It took six months before I laughed— *really* laughed—for the first time since she transitioned. And when it happened, instead of relief, I felt like I had done something terribly wrong.

It was just a small moment—so quick I barely remember what caused it. Maybe something my daughter said. Maybe a memory that caught me off guard. Maybe a silly video playing in the background. Whatever it was, the laugh escaped before I could stop it. A sound I hadn't heard from myself in months. A sound that should have felt healing.

But the moment it slipped out, the guilt came right behind it—sharp and immediate.

How could I laugh when she was gone?

How could joy still exist in a world where she didn't? How dare I allow myself even a second of lightness when everything inside me still felt so dark?

It was as if joy had become betrayal. As if my laughter meant I was moving on, forgetting, or leaving her behind. Grief will trick you like that—making you believe that healing is disloyalty.

In that moment, I realized grief wasn't just sadness. It was confusing. Conflict. A tug-of-war between wanting to honor her memory and wanting to feel alive again. That tiny laugh was a reminder that I was still human. That even in deep loss, small flickers of joy will try to break through. And that it's okay—pain and joy can coexist, even when your heart doubts it.

Then the day came when I had to clean out her storage unit, and it felt like opening a door I wasn't ready to walk through. Each box, each bag, each item carried her fingerprint—her handwriting on a label, her scent still clinging to a sweater, the quiet echo of her life in every corner. I found myself holding things longer than I needed to, stalling, because packing them away felt like packing her away. The guilt settled heavy in my chest—guilt for deciding what to keep, what to donate, what to let go of. Who was I to decide what stayed and what didn't? It felt like I was dismantling her life piece by piece, when all I wanted was one more day with her intact. That's what grief does. It warps your sense of what's allowed. You start to feel like any sign of happiness is a betrayal. Like if you start smiling again, you're leaving her behind. Like joy means forgetting. Like healing means dishonoring the depth of what you lost.

But that's not the truth. That's grief playing tricks on you.

Still, I wrestled with it—quietly. I'd go out with friends and come home hollow. I'd smile for pictures and then cry in the car. I'd post something positive on social media and immediately wonder if people thought I was "over it." I wasn't. Not even close. But I was learning how to carry it differently.

What they don't tell you about healing is that it comes with guilt.

Guilt for moving forward.

Guilt for taking care of yourself.

Guilt for laughing.

Guilt for planning a future she's not in.

Guilt for not crying every single day.

And even guilt for crying *too much*.

There is no winning with grief. Only walking through it.

And eventually, I had to ask myself: **Would my mom want me to suffer forever?**

I know her heart. And I know the answer.

She would want me to live.

To grow.

To keep loving.

To laugh loud and without apology.

To raise my daughter with joy—not just survival.

By the third year after her passing, I finally began giving myself permission—permission to enjoy moments without questioning whether I deserved them. Permission to laugh without feeling guilty. Permission to dance again. To dream again. To love again. I allowed myself to step back into life, not because the pain disappeared, but because I realized she would have wanted me to keep living, not just surviving.

I still carry her with me. That will never change. But I no longer carry her through sorrow alone. I carry her through celebration, too, and I always will.

She's in the meals I cook when people come over.

She's in the softness I offer others.

She's in the way I speak to my daughter when I'm tired but patient.

She's in the joy I let myself feel again.

Moving on isn't about forgetting her. It's about honoring her by living the kind of life she wanted for me.

And when the guilt still whispers—because it does—I remind myself:

This is love, too.

This laughter.

This forward motion.

This breath I'm still taking.

This life I'm still building.

She would be proud of me. I know she is, and your loved one is too.

My Precious Lessons

I've learned that guilt is often grief wearing a different face. It shows up when love has nowhere to land and tries to convince you that healing is betrayal. I learned that laughing doesn't erase the pain, and joy doesn't cancel the loss. Both can exist at the same time.

I also learned that moving forward is not the same as moving on. Moving forward means carrying my mother with me—into new moments, new memories, and new versions of myself. It means allowing life to continue without believing that doing so dishonors her memory.

Most importantly, I learned that guilt does not get to decide how I live. Love does.

Gems Along The Way

The things that helped me heal during my time of grief that may also help you are:

- **Remembering her lessons:** Reminding myself—again and again—of who my mother was and what she would want for me. She didn't raise me to suffer endlessly. She raised me to live fully, love deeply, and find joy even after hardship.

- **Releasing guilt:** I began speaking back to the guilt when it showed up. When it whispered that I was wrong for laughing, I reminded myself that laughter was once something she gave me freely. When it tried to convince me I was forgetting her, I grounded myself in the truth that she lives on through my actions, my compassion, and the way I love others.

- **Allowing myself to feel joy in small doses helped:** I didn't force happiness—I simply stopped blocking it when it arrived. Over time, I learned that honoring my mother didn't mean staying stuck in sorrow. It meant living the kind of life she hoped I would.

Journal to Healing

Take a moment to sit with what you've read in this chapter and reflect on your own journey. Allow the truth to gently rise to the surface. Let this be a space where your grief is allowed to exist—just as it is. In your journal, write your thoughts freely, openly, and honestly—without judgment, without pressure. There are no wrong answers here, only truth waiting to be realized.

1. When does guilt show up for you?

2. How can you honor your loved one?

3. What moments of joy have you questioned or pushed away because of grief?

4. What would your loved one say to you if they saw you holding yourself back from living?

5. How might joy be another way of honoring their love, rather than betraying it?

6. What is one small permission you can give yourself today—without guilt?

- THIRTEEN -

Honoring Her Life Every Day

G rief is part of love.
And so is remembrance.

There came a point in my journey where I realized something that quietly shifted everything: I wasn't just grieving her death—I was carrying her life forward. Her story didn't end the day she transitioned. It continued, in ways both visible and unseen, through the people she loved and the values she lived by.

My mother was a woman of quiet strength and consistent love. She didn't need applause to be powerful. She didn't need a stage to be impactful. Her presence spoke for itself. Her life touched people simply because of how she moved through the world—how she made space for others, how she showed up without needing recognition, how she loved with intention and depth.

And I knew I wanted to keep that going.

In the beginning, I thought honoring her would mean big gestures—events, foundations, speeches. I thought legacy had to be loud to be meaningful. And maybe those things still come in time. But what I've come to learn is that some of the most powerful ways I honor her are found in the smallest, quietest moments.

A thought.

A memory.

A pause when I feel her near.

Celebrating her on February 22nd, the day she transitioned, and on her birthday—not as days of only sadness, but as days of gratitude for having known her. Speaking her name in conversations so she's never erased. Smiling when someone says I sound like her, or move like her, or love like her—because those moments remind me that she is still here in ways that matter.

I see her in how I mother my daughter.

In how I offer grace to others when it would be easier to be guarded.

In how I tell the truth, even when my voice shakes.

In how I create space for healing—not just for myself, but for those around me.

I had to transition from *Being Anchored* by my mother to **Becoming My Own Anchor** and an anchor for others.

When I teach a young girl how to crochet, I'm honoring my mother's nurturing spirit—the way she believed in passing down patience, creativity, and care. When I speak life into a woman who feels like giving up, I'm echoing my mother's wisdom—the same words she once poured into me. When I protect my peace and walk away from chaos, I'm modeling her quiet power—the strength she carried without ever needing to announce it.

She didn't live a loud life, but she lived a meaningful one. And now, I get to continue it, piece by piece, choice by choice.

There are still days I ache. Days I wish I could call her just to hear her thoughts, her advice, her reassurance. Days I cry because I miss her hands, her scent, her way of making everything feel okay without even trying.

But I'm learning that I don't have to "get over" losing her.

I'm learning how to bring her with me.

Every act of kindness becomes a tribute.

Every prayer I whisper is a continuation.

Every brave step I take is a love letter to the woman who first taught me how to walk.

Honoring her life doesn't mean living in the past—it means letting her life echo through mine.

And the most beautiful part is this:

Now, when people see me …

When they feel warmth in my presence …

When they sense strength in my spirit …

They are seeing her, too.

She lives on in me.

And that is the most sacred honor of all.

My Precious Lessons

I've learned that honoring someone doesn't require perfection or grand displays—it requires presence. I learned that legacy isn't something you leave behind; it's something you live out. Carrying my mother forward has shown me that grief and purpose can exist side by side, and that remembrance can be a source of strength rather than pain.

I also learned that becoming an anchor for others doesn't mean losing myself—it means leading with compassion, boundaries, and purpose, just as she did.

Gems Along The Way

The things that helped me heal during my time of grief that may also help you are:

- **Shifting my perspective from loss to legacy:** Instead of asking how to survive without her, I began asking how to live because of her. Speaking her name, sharing her stories, and recognizing her influence in my own actions became sources of comfort rather than pain.

- **Incorporating rituals:** I created small, intentional rituals— honoring meaningful dates, passing on what she taught me, and choosing peace when chaos tried to pull me back in. Those moments helped me feel connected instead of separated. I realized that honoring her wasn't about staying rooted in grief, but about allowing her love to keep moving through me.

- **Grounding through service:** Serving others grounded me in ways I didn't expect. Teaching, nurturing, creating space for healing, and protecting my peace allowed me to feel close to her presence. Remembering her through love—rather than only through loss—softened my grief and transformed it into something purposeful.

Journal to Healing

Take a moment to sit with what you've read in this chapter and reflect on your own journey. Allow the truth to gently rise to the surface. Let this be a space where your grief is allowed to exist—just as it is. In your journal, write your thoughts freely, openly, and honestly—without judgment, without pressure. There are no wrong answers here, only truth waiting to be realized.

1. How do you honor your loved one in small, everyday ways?

2. What values or lessons did they pass down to you?

3. How can their life continue to live through your actions, words, or choices?

4. What would it look like to carry their love forward instead of holding your grief alone?

- FOURTEEN -

Light in the Shadows

H ealing doesn't mean forgetting.
And it doesn't mean you stop missing them.

It means you learn to live with the missing.

For a long time, I thought healing would look like finally feeling *better*. Like one day I'd wake up, and the grief would be gone, and I'd somehow return to the version of myself that existed before loss touched my life.

But that person no longer exists.

And I'm learning—that's okay.

Grief changed me. Loss reshaped the very core of my heart. It rearranged how I see the world, how I love, how I move through my days. At first, the pain felt unbearable—sharp, consuming, and endless. But with time, the weight began to soften. Not disappear, but ease. The edges dulled. The constant ache loosened its grip.

And little by little, light began to return.

Not in a flood.

Not all at once.

But in gentle glimpses—quiet flashes that reminded me hope still existed.

Like my daughter laughing in the kitchen, unaware that her joy was anchoring me.

Like a stranger holding the door open and smiling kindly on a day I almost stayed in bed.

Like sunlight pouring through my window, warming my face when I didn't think I had the strength to get up.

Like a familiar song that once made me cry now bringing a soft smile instead of tears.

The shadows didn't leave.

But I stopped being afraid of them.

Instead of hiding from the dark, I started looking for the light *inside* it. I began noticing the ways my mother still shows up. The ways I've grown. The strength I didn't know I carried. The softness that somehow survived everything I lost.

Grief taught me how to sit still with pain and not run from it.

It taught me how to live without answers and still keep going.

It taught me that healing isn't a destination—it's a choice I make again and again.

Some days, the weight still settles heavily on my chest, and I give myself permission to rest.

Other days, I feel full of purpose, energy, and clarity—and I run with it.

But no matter what kind of day it is, I know this now:

There is always light somewhere.

Even in the deepest shadows.

And sometimes … the light is me.

That's something I never would have said in the beginning. But now I can. Because I know that just by continuing to live—with love, intention, and hope—I am shining.

For my daughter.

For my partner.

For the people I serve.

For my mother.

And for the version of me who once believed she wouldn't survive this pain.

Every breath I take.

Every time I rise again.

Every moment I choose joy over despair.

It is a testament.

To her.

To love.

To resilience.

I used to think I had to wait for the pain to pass before I could live again.

Now I know—I can carry both.

Grief in one hand.

Gratitude in the other.

And in the middle of it all … a soft, growing light.

My Precious Lessons

I've learned that healing doesn't erase grief—it teaches you how to carry it with grace. I've learned that darkness and light are not opposites; they often exist together. Grief doesn't mean I am broken, and joy doesn't mean I've forgotten. I've learned that even when loss changes you forever, it doesn't strip you of purpose. Sometimes, it reveals it

Gems Along The Way

The things that helped me heal during my time of grief that may also help you are:

- **Small moments matter:** Allowing myself to notice the small moments, instead of waiting for big breakthroughs, helped. I stopped searching for a version of healing that looked perfect and began honoring the one that looked real. I paid attention to what softened my heart—laughter, nature, memories, faith, and connection.

- **Permission to feel:** Giving myself permission to feel both sadness and joy without guilt helped me breathe again. I learned to rest when I needed to and move forward when I could. Trusting that light would return—even slowly—helped me keep going on days when hope felt distant.

Journal to Healing

Take a moment to sit with what you've read in this chapter and reflect on your own journey. Allow the truth to gently rise to the surface. Let this be a space where your grief is allowed to exist—just as it is. In your journal, write your thoughts freely, openly, and honestly—without judgment, without pressure. There are no wrong answers here, only truth waiting to be realized.

1. Where have you noticed small glimpses of light in your grief?

2. What moments, people, or memories bring even a slight sense of warmth?

3. How do you respond to the shadows—do you fight them, or can you sit with them?

4. In what ways might *you* be the light, even on days you don't feel strong?

- FIFTEEN -

Life Goes On, So Will I

They say life goes on.
At first, I hated that phrase. It felt like betrayal. Like a reminder that the world kept turning while mine had stopped. I didn't want life to just "go on." I wanted it to pause, rewind, or at least acknowledge that something sacred had been lost.

But now? I hear those words differently.

Life goes on—and *so will I.*

Not the same. Not untouched. Not forgetting.

But continuing. Living. Becoming.

Grief carved something deep in me, something no one sees unless they know loss intimately. But it also made space—for truth, for softness, for deeper love.

I've grown in ways I never asked for.

I've found strength I never knew I'd need.

I've become more patient with others—and with myself.

I've learned to hold space for joy *and* sorrow, peace *and* pain.

I still miss my mother every single day.

But I no longer resist the ache.

Now, I let it move through me.

I let it remind me that I was loved that deeply.

Her absence sharpened my purpose.

Now, I mother with intention.

Now, I speak with courage.

Now, I create safe spaces for others who are hurting—because I know how isolating pain can feel.

Now, I'm a woman who knows what it means to lose ... and still choose to love again.

To believe again.

To breathe again.

This isn't the ending I would have chosen.

But I trust I'm still being led.

By God.

By purpose.

By the whisper of her love that still lives in me.

Life goes on.

It won't look like what it once was.

And I may not always move forward with ease.

But I will move forward—with grace. With faith. With her name etched in every step.

Because I carry her.

Because I am her.

And because I am still becoming.

So, if you ask me now, 4 years later, after all I've walked through, what I've learned?

I'd say this:

Grief will shake you.

Loss will change you.

But love will rebuild you—softly, slowly, fully.

And yes ...

Life goes on.

So will I.

And, so will you.

My Precious Lessons

I've learned that grief doesn't end—it evolves. It changes shape as you do. I learned that continuing to live doesn't mean I've forgotten who I lost; it means I'm honoring them through how I show up now.

I learned that becoming someone new after loss isn't betrayal—it's growth. That softness isn't weakness, and resilience doesn't require hardening. I learned that love doesn't disappear with death—it deepens, stretches, and finds new ways to live.

Most of all, I learned that I am allowed to keep becoming—even after my heart has been broken.

Gems Along The Way

The things that helped me heal during my time of grief that may also help you are:

- **Move on:** What helped me was releasing the idea that I had to "move on" and allowing myself to move *with* my grief instead. I stopped resisting the ache and let it guide me toward purpose, compassion, and deeper connection.

- **Trust Faith:** Faith helped me trust that even when the path didn't make sense, I wasn't walking alone. Remembering my mother through intention—through how I love, speak, mother, and serve—helped me feel connected instead of separated.

- **Live:** I learned that choosing to live again wasn't dishonoring her. It was honoring everything she poured into me.

Journal to Healing

Take a moment to sit with what you've read in this chapter and reflect on your own journey. Allow the truth to gently rise to the surface. Let this be a space where your grief is allowed to exist—just as it is. In your journal, write your thoughts freely, openly, and honestly—without judgment, without pressure. There are no wrong answers here, only truth waiting to be realized.

1. What does "life goes on" mean to you right now?

2. In what ways have you changed since your loss?

3. Where do you see love still rebuilding you?

4. What parts of you are still becoming?

5. How can you honor your loved one as you continue forward?

The Journey Continues

Grief doesn't end. It evolves.

When I first lost my mother on February 22, 2022—a day we called "Love Day"—I thought the world had stopped. Everything around me kept moving, but I felt frozen in a moment that shattered something deep inside me. I was a daughter with no roadmap, a mother trying to be strong, and a woman aching to understand how to go on.

And still ... I went on.

Writing this book wasn't just about telling my story—it was about breathing again. It was about making space for pain, reflection, faith, and the kind of growth that only comes through walking through fire and deciding to keep walking.

If you've made it this far, I want to say: *thank you*. Thank you for trusting me to walk beside you. Thank you for showing up—for yourself, your healing, your peace. I hope this book reminded you that it's okay to fall apart and rise again, one breath, one prayer, one page at a time.

Grief changes you. But you are not broken. You are being rebuilt. Stronger. Softer. Wiser. More compassionate.

I carry my mother with me in every chapter of my life now—in the quiet moments, in the laughter of my daughter, in the lessons I pass on. Her love didn't die. It transformed. And it lives through me.

As you continue your own journey, I leave you with this:

Hold onto faith, even when it's small.

Give yourself grace, even when you don't understand your tears.

And remember—you are never alone in this.

This isn't the end. It's a continuation.

The healing doesn't stop here. It deepens.

With love and hope,

Carin Seals

Acknowledgements

Nila Elaine, my daughter, my heart, my onlyest, I understand the pain you feel in losing your Nanny; I felt that same pain at the very same age. May you always know that she is forever with you, living in your heart. Hold tightly to the memories you shared, the pictures you took together, and cherish the words she spoke to you. They will continue to guide you, comfort you, and remind you that her love is forever present. On the days you miss her most, talk to her. She hears you. And on the days your heart feels heavy, rest in mine. I am here, always loving you, always walking with you. Love Mom

Angela, thank you for being by my side during the hardest months before my mother's transition. You stepped in to care for my mother as if she were your own. You will forever be her best tea maker! Thank you for your unconditional love. You held me up when I could no longer stand, wiped my tears until they ran dry, and cried with me in those quiet moments when I broke in the middle of the night. You saw me at my lowest and still pushed me to finish this book when I couldn't see the end for myself. I am forever grateful for your partnership, your presence, and your unwavering love.

Debbie Belnavis-Brimble of Capture Your Brilliance, thank you for being my visionary and bringing my story to life. You pushed me to dig deeper because you knew there was more that needed to be told. Your patience and grace gave me the strength to keep going. In the moments when I could give only 20%, you stepped in and carried the remaining 80%. I am forever grateful that our paths aligned at exactly the right time. Our work together is just beginning!

Ms. Heidi Siebels, thank you for believing in me and for taking the time to reach out to assist with my editing. As my ninth grade teacher, you saw potential in me when I didn't fully see it in myself, and that has stayed with me all these years. You were an amazing teacher with a truly beautiful soul, and I am deeply grateful for your support!

My Siblings, Shonda, Monique, and Ryan Seals, we all hold a piece of mommy within us, and together we carry her love forward. #WeAllWeGot, Love you all!

Louis Hargrove (Dad), I love you, and your love will always be enough.

My Aunts, Danita Dillard, Charlene Seals, Claudette Tarrent, and Kizzy Brown, thank you for the shared memories, the stories, and the love that keeps her presence close. Love you

Richard Seals (Unc PT), love you and thank you and Aunt Camilia for loving Nila like your own.

Bonus Aunts, Kysha Payne & Beverly Shepheard, thank you for continuing to show up for us. Love you

Nanny Audrey, thank you for opening your doors and heart to us. You are the true MVP! Love you

My Mother's Bonus Sisters, Melinda Allen & Freda Hall. You two showed up for my mother and her children in ways that we will forever cherish. Love you

My Friend Circle, I remember breaking down at the graveside, and when I turned around, I saw love. Thank you all for standing in the gap and showing up for me on that day — and every day after when I needed you most. Every phone call answered, every laugh shared, every tear you heard—in silence or out loud—has not gone unnoticed. I love you all.

Quinn Conyers, Lauren Drumgoole, Marquisha Myers, Andrea Parker-Brown, Nyeemah Seals, Lamesha Miles, Tianna Glenn-Wright (Kim), Hasinah Shabazz, Jennel Datil, Chante' Espinosa, Taya Smith, Audrisha Springer, Kristen Mitchell, Leah Walker, Neya Chance and Alesha Willingham.

Angela "Phree" Wright, Thank you, sis, for always pushing me to keep going. Your obedience to God and your commitment to helping others find freedom have always been done selflessly. You thought you only had one more person to help in gaining their freedom, not realizing that person was me. As soon as I was released, your paperwork was signed. I thank God for aligning our paths at the exact moment I needed it most. Love you.

Cousin Derrick, when I called, you showed up for me every time. Thank you for taking that trip to PA and supporting me. Love you Cuz

Special thank you to Gov Con.

www.ingramcontent.com/pod-product-compliance
Lightning Source LLC
Chambersburg PA
CBHW070459090426
42735CB00012B/2613